Kaplan Publishing are constantly finding new ways to support students looking for exam success and our online re extra dimension to your studies.

This book comes with free MyKaplan online study anytime, anywhere. **This free online separately and is included in the price of**

C000132918

Having purchased this book, you have access to the following online study materials:

CONTENT	AAT	
	Text	Kit
Electronic version of the book	✓	✓
Knowledge Check tests with instant answers	✓	
Mock assessments online	✓	✓
Material updates	✓	✓

How to access your online resources

Kaplan Financial students will already have a MyKaplan account and these extra resources will be available to you online. You do not need to register again, as this process was completed when you enrolled. If you are having problems accessing online materials, please ask your course administrator.

If you are not studying with Kaplan and did not purchase your book via a Kaplan website, to unlock your extra online resources please go to www.mykaplan.co.uk/add-online-resources (even if you have set up an account and registered books previously). You will then need to enter the ISBN number (on the title page and back cover) and the unique pass key number contained in the scratch panel below to gain access. You will also be required to enter additional information during this process to set up or confirm your account details.

If you purchased through the Kaplan Publishing website you will automatically receive an e-mail invitation to MyKaplan. Please register your details using this email to gain access to your content. If you do not receive the e-mail or book content, please contact Kaplan Publishing.

Your Code and Information

This code can only be used once for the registration of one book online. This registration and your online content will expire when the final sittings for the examinations covered by this book have taken place. Please allow one hour from the time you submit your book details for us to process your request.

Please scratch the film to access your unique code.

Please be aware that this code is case-sensitive and you will need to include the dashes within the passcode, but not when entering the ISBN.

KAPLAN

PUBLISHING

THE BUSINESS ENVIRONMENT SYNOPTIC

STUDY TEXT

Qualifications and Credit Framework

Q22 Level 2 Certificate in Accounting

This Study Text supports study for the following AAT qualifications:

AAT Level 2 Certificate in Accounting

AAT Level 2 Certificate in Bookkeeping

AAT Certificate in Accounting at SCQF Level 6

KAPLAN PUBLISHING'S STATEMENT OF PRINCIPLES

LINGUISTIC DIVERSITY, EQUALITY AND INCLUSION

We are committed to diversity, equality and inclusion and strive to deliver content that all users can relate to.

We are here to make a difference to the success of every learner.

Clarity, accessibility and ease of use for our learners are key to our approach.

We will use contemporary examples that are rich, engaging and representative of a diverse workplace.

We will include a representative mix of race and gender at the various levels of seniority within the businesses in our examples to support all our learners in aspiring to achieve their potential within their chosen careers.

Roles played by characters in our examples will demonstrate richness and diversity by the use of different names, backgrounds, ethnicity and gender, with a mix of sexuality, relationships and beliefs where these are relevant to the syllabus.

It must always be obvious who is being referred to in each stage of any example so that we do not detract from clarity and ease of use for each of our learners.

We will actively seek feedback from our learners on our approach and keep our policy under continuous review. If you would like to provide any feedback on our linguistic approach, please use this form (you will need to enter the link below into your browser).

https://forms.gle/U8oR3abiPpGRDY158

We will seek to devise simple measures that can be used by independent assessors to randomly check our success in the implementation of our Linguistic Equality, Diversity and Inclusion Policy.

British Library Cataloguing-in-Publication Data

A catalogue record for this book is available from the British Library.

Published by
Kaplan Publishing UK
Unit 2, The Business Centre
Molly Millars Lane
Wokingham
Berkshire
RG41 2QZ

ISBN 978-1-83996-041-3

Printed and bound in Great Britain.

We are grateful to HM Revenue and Customs for the provision of tax forms, which are Crown Copyright and are reproduced here with kind permission from the Office of Public Sector Information.

CONTENTS

KAPLAN PUBLISHING

INTRODUCTION

HOW TO USE THESE MATERIALS

These Kaplan Publishing learning materials have been carefully designed to make your learning experience as easy as possible and to give you the best chance of success in your AAT assessments.

They contain a number of features to help you in the study process.

The sections on the Unit Guide, the Assessment and Study Skills should be read before you commence your studies.

They are designed to familiarise you with the nature and content of the assessment and to give you tips on how best to approach your studies.

STUDY TEXT

This study text has been specially prepared for the revised AAT qualification introduced in September 2022.

It is written in a practical and interactive style:

- key terms and concepts are clearly defined

- all topics are illustrated with practical examples with clearly worked solutions based on sample tasks provided by the AAT in the new examining style

- frequent activities throughout the chapters ensure that what you have learnt is regularly reinforced

- 'pitfalls' and 'examination tips' help you avoid common mistakes and focus on what is required to perform well in your examination.

ICONS

The study chapters include the following icons throughout.

They are designed to assist you in your studies by identifying key definitions and the points at which you can test yourself on the knowledge gained.

 Definition

These sections explain important areas of knowledge which must be understood and reproduced in an assessment.

 Example

The illustrative examples can be used to help develop an understanding of topics before attempting the test your understanding exercises.

 Test your understanding

These are exercises which give the opportunity to assess your understanding of all the assessment areas.

Quality and accuracy are of the utmost importance to us so if you spot an error in any of our products, please send an email to mykaplanreporting@kaplan.com with full details, or follow the link to the feedback form in MyKaplan.

Our Quality Co-ordinator will work with our technical team to verify the error and take action to ensure it is corrected in future editions.

KAPLAN PUBLISHING

Progression

There are two elements of progression that we can measure: first, how quickly students move through individual topics within a subject; and second, how quickly they move from one course to the next. We know that there is an optimum for both, but it can vary from subject to subject and from student to student. However, using data and our experience of student performance over many years, we can make some generalisations.

A fixed period of study set out at the start of a course with key milestones is important. This can be within a subject, for example, 'I will finish this topic by 30 June', or for overall achievement, such as, 'I want to be qualified by the end of next year'.

Your qualification is cumulative, as earlier papers provide a foundation for your subsequent studies, so do not allow there to be too big a gap between one subject and another.

We know that exams encourage techniques that lead to some degree of short-term retention, the result being that you will simply forget much of what you have already learned unless it is refreshed (look up 'Ebbinghaus Forgetting Curve' for more details on this). This makes it more difficult as you move from one subject to another: not only will you have to learn the new subject, you will also have to relearn all the underpinning knowledge. This is very inefficient and slows down your overall progression, which makes it more likely you may not succeed at all.

In addition, delaying your studies slows your path to qualification which can have negative impacts on your career, such as postponing the opportunity to apply for higher level positions and therefore higher pay.

You can use the following diagram which shows the whole structure of your qualification, to help you keep track of your progress.

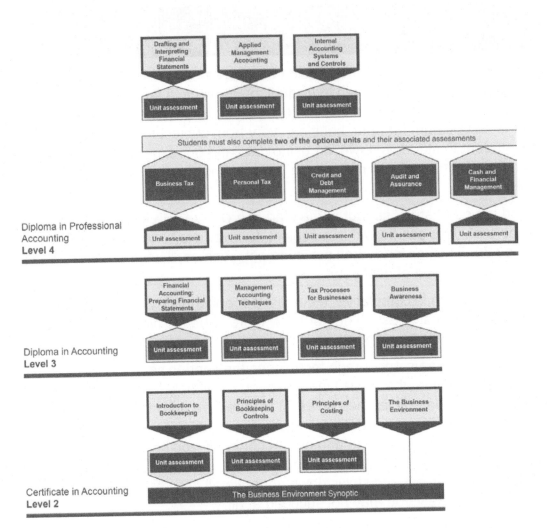

SYNOPTIC ASSESSMENT GUIDE

Introduction

AAT Q22 introduces a Synoptic Assessment, which students must complete if they are to achieve the appropriate qualification. In the case of the Level 2 Certificate in Accounting, students must pass all of the mandatory assessments and the Synoptic Assessment to achieve the qualification.

As a Synoptic Assessment is attempted following completion of individual units, it draws upon knowledge and understanding from those units. It may be appropriate for students to retain their study materials for individual units until they have successfully completed the Synoptic Assessment for that qualification.

All units within the Level 2 Certificate in Accounting are mandatory. Three units are assessed individually in end-of-unit assessments, but this qualification also includes a synoptic assessment, sat towards the end of the qualification, which draws on and assesses knowledge and understanding from across the qualification.

- Introduction to Bookkeeping – end-of-unit assessment
- Principles of Bookkeeping Controls – end-of-unit assessment
- Principles of Costing – end-of-unit assessment
- The Business Environment – assessed within the synoptic assessment only

Note that Principles of Costing is a unit assessment only and is not assessed as part of the Synoptic Assessment.

Scope of content

The synoptic assessment will ask you to apply knowledge and skills gained across the qualification in an integrated way, within a workplace context. Scenarios will change over time to ensure the validity of the assessment.

To complete this synoptic assessment effectively you will need to know and understand the following:

Assessment objective 1	Demonstrate an understanding of the different business types and their functions
Related learning outcomes	**The Business Environment** LO4 Understand the impact of setting up different types of business entity LO5 Understand the finance function within an organisation
Assessment objective 2	Demonstrate an understanding of the finance function, its information requirements and sources, and its role in the wider organisation
Related learning outcomes	**The Business Environment** LO5 Understand the finance function within an organisation LO6 Produce work in appropriate formats and communicate effectively LO7 Understand the importance of information to business operations

KAPLAN PUBLISHING

Assessment objective 3	Demonstrate an understanding of corporate social responsibility (CSR), ethics and sustainability
Related learning outcomes	**The Business Environment** LO3 Understand the principles of corporate social responsibility (CSR), ethics and sustainability
Assessment objective 4	Process bookkeeping transactions and communicate information
Related learning outcomes	**Introduction to Bookkeeping** LO1 Understand to set up bookkeeping systems LO2 Process customer transactions LO3 Process supplier transactions **The Business Environment** LO6 Produce work in appropriate formats and communicate effectively
Assessment objective 5	Produce and reconcile control accounts and use journals to correct errors
Related learning outcomes	**Principles of Bookkeeping Controls** LO1 Use control accounts LO2 Reconcile a bank statement with the cash book LO3 Use the journal
Assessment objective 6	Demonstrate an understanding of the principles of contract law
Related learning outcome	**The Business Environment** LO1 Understand the principles of contract law

Assessment objective 7	Demonstrate an understanding of bookkeeping systems, receipts and payments, and the importance of information and data security
Related learning outcomes	**The Business Environment** LO7 Understand the importance of information to business operations **Introduction to Bookkeeping** LO1 Understand how to set up bookkeeping systems LO2 Process customer transactions LO3 Process supplier transactions **Principles of Bookkeeping Controls** LO1 Use control accounts LO2 Reconcile a bank statement with the cash book LO3 Use the journal
Assessment objective 8	Demonstrate an understanding of the global business environment
Related learning outcome	**The Business Environment** LO2 Understand the external business environment

THE ASSESSMENT

Test specification for this synoptic assessment

Assessment type	Marking type	Duration of exam
Computer-based synoptic assessment	Partially computer/ partially human marked	2 hours

The following weighting is based upon the AAT Qualification Specification documentation which may be subject to variation.

Assessment objective	Weighting
A01	
Demonstrate an understanding of the different business types and their functions	10%
A02	
Demonstrate an understanding of the finance function, its information requirements and sources, and its role in the wider organisation	13%
A03	
Demonstrate an understanding of corporate social responsibility (CSR), ethics and sustainability	14%
A04	
Process bookkeeping transactions and communicate information	22%
A05	
Produce and reconcile control accounts, and use journals to correct errors	10%
A06	
Demonstrate an understanding of the principles of contract law	7%

A07

Demonstrate an understanding of bookkeeping systems, receipts and payments, and the importance of information and data security	10%

A08

Demonstrate an understanding of the global business environment	14%
Total	**100%**

KAPLAN PUBLISHING

STUDY SKILLS

Preparing to study

Devise a study plan

Determine which times of the week you will study.

Split these times into sessions of at least one hour for study of new material. Any shorter periods could be used for revision or practice.

Put the times you plan to study onto a study plan for the weeks from now until the assessment and set yourself targets for each period of study – in your sessions make sure you cover the whole course, activities and the associated questions in the workbook at the back of the manual.

If you are studying more than one unit at a time, try to vary your subjects as this can help to keep you interested and see subjects as part of wider knowledge.

When working through your course, compare your progress with your plan and, if necessary, re-plan your work (perhaps including extra sessions) or, if you are ahead, do some extra revision/practice questions.

Effective studying

Active reading

You are not expected to learn the text by rote, rather, you must understand what you are reading and be able to use it to pass the assessment and develop good practice.

A good technique is to use SQ3Rs – Survey, Question, Read, Recall, Review:

1   **Survey the chapter**

     Look at the headings and read the introduction, knowledge, skills and content, so as to get an overview of what the chapter deals with.

2   **Question**

     Whilst undertaking the survey ask yourself the questions you hope the chapter will answer for you.

3   Read

Read through the chapter thoroughly working through the activities and, at the end, making sure that you can meet the learning objectives highlighted on the first page.

4   Recall

At the end of each section and at the end of the chapter, try to recall the main ideas of the section/chapter without referring to the text. This is best done after short break of a couple of minutes after the reading stage.

5   Review

Check that your recall notes are correct.

You may also find it helpful to reread the chapter to recap the topic(s) it deals with as a whole.

Note taking

Taking notes is a useful way of learning, but do not simply copy out the text.

The notes must:

- be in your own words
- be concise
- cover the key points
- be well organised
- be modified as you study further chapters in this text or in related ones.

Trying to summarise a chapter without referring to the text can be a useful way of determining which areas you know and which you don't.

Three ways of taking notes

1   Summarise the key points of a chapter

2   Make linear notes

A list of headings, subdivided with subheadings listing the key points.

Use different colours to highlight key points and keep topic areas together.

Use plenty of space to make your notes easy to use.

3 Try a diagrammatic form

The most common of which is a mind map.

To make a mind map, put the main heading in the centre of the paper and put a circle around it.

Draw lines radiating from this to the main subheadings which again have circles around them.

Continue the process from the subheadings to sub-subheadings.

Highlighting and underlining

You may find it useful to underline or highlight key points in your study text – but do be selective.

You may also wish to make notes in the margins.

Revision phase

Kaplan has produced materials specifically designed for your final examination preparation for this synoptic assessment.

These include pocket revision notes and a bank of revision questions specifically in the style of the new syllabus.

Further guidance on how to approach the final stage of your studies is given in these materials.

Further reading

In addition to this text, you should also read the 'Accounting Technician' magazine every month to keep abreast of any guidance from the examiners.

THE BUSINESS ENVIRONMENT – UNIT GUIDE

The Business Environment is assessed as part of the synoptic assessment only and not as a stand-alone unit.

Purpose of the unit

This unit will help students to develop the professional skills and behaviours needed in the workplace. Learners will be able to work independently or as part of a team. While this unit is set in the context of the finance function, these skills are transferable to many other working environments.

Students will understand the work of the finance function and why that work is important to an organisation. They will understand that finance employees require more than numerical skills: they also need interpersonal and written communication skills. Students will learn the importance of being an effective employee, what this means, and how to work as part of a finance team. Students will be able to identify activities that develop current skills and knowledge, and those that will help them achieve future career aspirations. Students will understand how to ensure data security and the importance of maintaining confidentiality of information. Students will understand why corporate social responsibility is important and what actions individuals can take to ensure that they behave ethically and support sustainability.

The communication and numeracy skills included within this unit will be beneficial to those studying all AAT qualifications. The written communication skills element of this unit will prepare students for work and further study by developing their reading and writing skills. The basic numerical functions covered in this unit are important in all financial computations and, as such, students who successfully complete this unit should have an increased confidence in dealing with financial computations.

The Business Environment is a **mandatory unit** in this qualification.

Learning outcomes

On completion of this unit the learner will be able to:

- Understand the principles of contract law.

- Understand the external business environment.

- Understand the key principles of corporate social responsibility (CSR), ethics and sustainability.

- Understand the impact of setting up different types of business entity.

- Understand the finance function within an organisation.

- Produce work in appropriate formats and communicate effectively.

- Understand the importance of information to business operations.

Knowledge

To perform this unit effectively you will need to know and understand the following:

Chapter

1 Understand the principles of contract law

1.1 The different classifications of law   1

Learners need to understand:

- the principles of:

    - common law and equity

    - public law and private law

    - criminal law and civil law

1.2 The main sources of law   1

Learners need to understand:

- the development of law by the courts, tribunals and parliament.

Chapter

1.3 Key features of contracts   2

Learners need to know:

- the meaning of invitation to treat, offer and termination

- the meaning and consequences of acceptance

- the meaning of and the need for consideration

- capacity and legality (valid, void, voidable contracts)

- the meaning of discharge of contract:

    - by performance

    - by breach.

1.4 Remedies available for breach of contract   2

Learners need to understand:

- the consequences of being in breach of contract through:

    - damages

    - equitable remedies.

2   Understand the external business environment

2.1 The economic environment   3

Learners need to understand:

- the micro-economic environment:

    - the forces of supply and demand on pricing and output

- the profit motive of business

- that businesses face uncertainty and risk

- that businesses operate in a global business environment.

Chapter

2.2   Government control of the economy   3

Learners need to understand:

- how government controls the economy

- the key principles of an effective tax system:
    - equity
    - certainty
    - convenience
    - economy
    - fairness
    - transparency

- how government raises finances through the tax system from:
    - individuals
    - businesses
    - indirect taxes

- the impact of government on interest rates, levels of employment and consumer spending.

2.3   The competitive environment   3

Learners need to understand:

- how the competitive global market may affect a business

- how changes in exchange rates may change business costs

- the uncertainty and risks faced by business in the global market

- the benefits and disadvantages to a business of trading internationally.

Chapter

3 **Understand the principles of corporate social responsibility (CSR), ethics and sustainability**

3.1 Corporate social responsibilities of a business   4

Learners need to understand:

- the objective of CSR

- the involvement of internal and external stakeholders

- how CSR responsibilities change over time.

3.2 Sustainability and the environment   4

Learners need to understand:

- the responsibility of business with respect to sustainability

- the principle of triple bottom line reporting

- there may be a trade-off between sustainability and profit

- how businesses respond to changes in the environment to succeed in the long term.

3.3 The fundamental principles of ethics for accounting technicians   4

Learners need to know:

- the five fundamental principles of ethics

   – confidentiality

   – professional behaviour

   – professional competence and due care

   – integrity

   – objectivity.

Chapter

4   Understand the impact of setting up different types of business entity

4.1   Models of business ownership   5

Learners need to understand:

- the entity concept

- the different legal structures that businesses adopt:

  - sole trader

  - partnership

  - company

  - not-for-profit organisation

- that ownership of a business can be separate from the management and control of a business

- the types of tax applicable to individuals, partnerships and companies:

  - income tax

  - PAYE

  - corporation tax

  - VAT

- the concept of limited liability and its effect

- the key features of each legal structure:

  - control

  - management

  - sources of finance

  - liability

  - distribution of profit.

Chapter

4.2   The legal administration of a business   5

Learners need to know:

- for sole traders and companies:

  – the statutory books that must be kept

  – the accounting records that must be kept

  – the tax records that must be kept

  – the annual financial statements that must be filed

  – the annual returns that must be filed

  – the electronic filing requirements.

4.3   Business formation   5

Learners need to know:

- how sole traders, partnerships and limited companies are formed

- the benefits and limitations of using 'off the shelf' companies

- why some companies may use pre-incorporation contracts

- the implications of business name:

  – what names can and cannot be used

  – rules about similar and misleading names

  – where names to be displayed.

Chapter

5 Understand the finance function within an organisation

5.1 The different functions of a business   6

Learners need to know:

- the different functions of a business:
    - operations/production
    - sales and marketing
    - finance
    - human resources
    - information technology
    - distribution and logistics

- the role each function plays in contributing to business success

- the interconnected nature of technology to support each function

- that these functions may be combined in smaller organisations.

5.2 The role of the finance function   6

Learners need to know:

- the role of the finance function:
    - responsibility for the production of statutory financial statements
    - providing a service (information, support, advice and guidance) to both internal and external stakeholders

- the relationship and interaction between finance and other functions of a business

- how processes within the finance function may be outsourced (e.g. payroll).

Chapter

5.3 How the finance team contributes to the success of an organisation — 6

Learners need to know:

- the importance of establishing effective business relationships
- the principles of effective communication:
    - content is written clearly, complete, accurate, timely and concise
    - meets the needs of the recipient
    - appropriate medium is used in a suitable environment
- how actions of finance staff support efficient working practices, solvency and long-term financial stability, legal and regulatory compliance
- the importance to an organisation's survival of remaining solvent and managing funds effectively
- the different types of policies and procedures affecting finance staff:
    - finance function-specific
    - organisation-wide
- the role of finance in CSR reporting.

6 Produce work in appropriate formats and communicate effectively

6.1 Sources of information — 7

Learners need to know:

- the difference between valid and invalid sources of information
- the difference between primary and secondary sources
- the benefits of obtaining information from more than one source
- the importance of recognising sources when producing information.

Learners need to be able to:

- choose information for a specific purpose.

KAPLAN PUBLISHING

6.2   Communicate information

Learners need to understand:

- the importance of effective note-taking and documenting key pieces of information:

    – when dealing with customers

    – during meetings (one-to-ones with line manager; team)

- the features of business communications:

    – business letters

    – emails

    – formal business reports

    – spreadsheets

    – social media communications

    – intranet

- the influence and impact of inappropriate social media postings

- the consequences of inappropriate information sharing.

Learners need to be able to:

- produce written communication using acceptable business language that is clear, structured and follows a logical progression:

    – business letters

    – emails

- recognise the impact and consequences of ineffective or inappropriate communication.

Chapter

6.3 Plan workload to meet the needs of the organisation   7

Learners need to understand:

- the importance of communicating with others whilst undertaking a task or if deadlines may not be met

- how to prioritise workloads based on urgency and importance

- the importance of meeting agreed deadlines and adhering to working practices

- the impact on others of not completing specified tasks.

Learners need to be able to:

- plan workload:
    - prioritise
    - monitor
    - review.

7 Understand the importance of information to business operations

7.1 The role of information in the work of the finance   8
function

Learners need to understand:

- the importance of providing useful information

- the characteristics of useful information:
    - comparable
    - consistent
    - understandable
    - relevant and reliable
    - timely

- the types of information and documentation received by the finance function:
    - budgetary
    - inventory control and costing information

Chapter

- – information from suppliers and customers

- – purchase orders

- – remittance advice

- – statements

- – supplier invoices

- – credit notes

- the types of information and documentation produced by the finance function:

  - – information to help management decision making

  - – budgetary information

  - – cash information

  - – taxation information

  - – information for suppliers and customers

  - – sales invoices

  - – credit notes

  - – statements.

7.2 The importance of data and information security   8

Learners need to know:

- why it is important to ensure the security of data and information

- why it is important to maintain privacy and confidentiality

- the implications for the organisation if data and information is not secure

- how data and information is retained securely: using passwords, archiving, backups and restricting access

- the importance of cybersecurity.

Delivering this unit

This unit has the following links across the AAT Level 2 Certificate in Accounting.

Unit name	Content links	Suggested order of delivery
Introduction to Bookkeeping	Numerical skills, communication of information and professional behaviour may be linked with Introduction to Bookkeeping.	Introduction to Bookkeeping might be delivered before, at the same time as or after The Business Environment. It is recommended that the synoptic assessment is only attempted after the contributing units are completed, although this is not compulsory.
Principles of Bookkeeping Controls	Numerical skills, communication of information and professional behaviour may be linked with Principles of Bookkeeping Controls.	Principles of Bookkeeping Controls might be delivered before, at the same time as or after The Business Environment. It is recommended that the synoptic assessment is only attempted after the contributing units are completed, although this is not compulsory.

The English legal system

1

Introduction

The AAT Business Environment unit introduces some of the main areas of business and company law that are relevant to the work of accountants. The purpose of the unit is to introduce some key aspects of commercial law and to demonstrate how the law affects the role of the professional accountant on a daily basis.

This unit also provides practical knowledge about the law that is useful in personal as well as work situations.

ASSESSMENT CRITERIA
1.1 The different classifications of law
1.2 The main sources of law

CONTENTS	
1	Sources of law
2	Case law and judicial precedent
3	Statute law
4	Public law and private law
5	Criminal law and civil law

1 Sources of law

1.1 What is law?

Definition

Law: The principles and regulations established in a community by some authority and applicable to its people whether in the form of legislation or of custom and policies recognised and enforced by judicial decision.

1.2 Sources of law

There are two main sources of law in the English legal system:

- **Case law** – law which has been developed over time by judges when deciding the outcome of cases brought before the courts. This law has evolved through the **common law** and **equity** systems.

- **Statute law** – laws made by Parliament through **direct legislation and delegated legislation**.

This chapter will explain these sources and summarise the court structure.

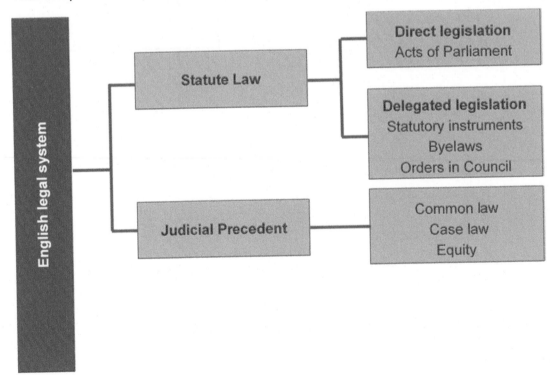

Test your understanding 1

Identify which of the following are sources of law in the English legal system.

Tick all that apply.

	Correct?
US Federal Law	
AAT conceptual framework	
UK common law	
Acts of Parliament	

2 Case law and judicial precedent

2.1 Common law

The English common law legal system evolved during the Middle Ages when the monarchy established a court system to unite both the country and its laws. Generally agreed local customs were absorbed into a body of law which could be applied to all the country: **the common law**.

One of the main features of common law is that it is based on **judicial precedent**.

2.2 What is judicial precedent?

The common law system developed in England and followed in many other countries follows the principle of **judicial precedent**.

 Definition

Judicial precedent is the system, adopted by judges, of following the decisions made in previous, similar cases.

Some precedents (previous decisions) are binding (they must be followed), whereas others are merely persuasive (the judge in a later case may choose not to follow them). This is examined further in a later section.

2.3   Equity

As common law courts developed, there was an increasing need for more formality. Technical requirements intensified and disputes could only be heard if they satisfied the correct legal process. This was seen to be rigid and inflexible. Also, under the common law system the only remedy available to claimants was **damages** (monetary compensation).

Courts of Equity were developed to run in parallel with the common law courts to apply principles of fairness and equity to individual cases and provide alternative remedies where monetary compensation was not appropriate.

Therefore, equity is both more flexible than common law and more concerned with **fairness**.

Whilst common law and equity courts have now merged and follow the system of judicial precedent, in the event of a conflict between equity and the common law, equity always takes precedence.

2.4   Remedies

 Definition

Damages are the monetary compensation awarded by a court to an individual who has suffered the wrongful conduct of another party. They are a common law remedy.

Equitable remedies are awarded where it is considered that a monetary compensation would not be appropriate. As such, they can provide greater flexibility and are discretionary.

Examples

Equitable remedies:

Specific Performance	The defendant is ordered to carry out their contractual duties.
Injunction	A court order requiring a person to do or cease to do a specific action.
Rescission	The cancellation of a contract.

Example

An example of specific performance being used in practice:

George agrees to sell Romauld a painting for £500.

George then discovers that the painting is actually worth £5,000.

George then refuses to complete the sale.

As the painting is a unique item that he cannot acquire elsewhere, Romauld could seek a court order for specific performance against George that orders George to sell the painting to him at the agreed £500 price.

2.5　Establishing judicial precedent

The system of following the decisions made in previous cases is called the doctrine of **judicial precedent**.

- Some precedents are **binding** (meaning they **must** be followed in later cases).

- Others are merely **persuasive** (meaning that a judge in a later case **may** choose to follow it but is not bound to do so).

There are three factors to be considered in deciding whether a precedent is binding or persuasive:

- the hierarchy of the courts

- ratio decidendi and obiter dicta

- the material facts of the case.

The hierarchy of the courts

As a general rule, the precedents of higher courts bind lower courts, but not vice versa. The court structure is examined further in section 4.

Ratio decidendi and obiter dicta

Not everything said in court is binding in later cases. In court judgements, a distinction needs to be made between the **ratio decidendi** (the reason for the decision) and **obiter dicta** – another remark made in passing (literally, 'things said along the way').

Definition

Ratio decidendi is the principle of law on which the decision is based, or the reason for deciding. It forms a binding precedent which can be carried down to determine future similar cases.

Obiter dicta is a comment or speculation made by the judge on aspects of the case. For example, the judge may discuss situations if the facts of the case were different or make more general legal comments.

Facts of the case

In order for a precedent to be binding on a judge in a later case, the material facts of the two cases must be the same. If they are significantly different, the precedent will be persuasive rather than binding.

When is a precedent not binding?

A precedent is not binding where it:

- has been overruled by a higher court.
- has been overruled by statute (i.e. legislation) – see further below.
- was made without proper care (per incuriam). This is when a decision of a court is held to be wrongly decided because the judge was misinformed of the law. A judgment per incuriam is not binding and has no authority.
- can be distinguished from the earlier case, i.e. the material facts differ.

In summary, a previous case is only binding in a later case if the earlier decision was made by a higher level court, the legal principle involved is the same and the facts are similar.

3 Statute law

3.1 What is statute law?

Statute law is law made by Parliament to regulate behaviour within a society.

 Example

Betty is driving on a road with a speed limit of 50 miles per hour. However, she is late for work and in a rush. She therefore decides to increase her speed to 70 miles per hour.

A police officer stops her and she is given a speeding ticket. Betty has broken a vehicle and traffic law (Road Traffic Offenders Act 1988). This Act was established as a statute, or a law that is formally written and enacted, having passed through the legislature (Parliament).

As a result, the law Betty broke was a **statutory law**.

3.2 Direct legislation

Parliament is the supreme legal authority in the UK and only Parliament has the authority to enact any law it wishes.

Parliament makes new laws, holds the power to set taxes and debates the issues of the day. The House of Commons (which is elected by the public) and the House of Lords (not elected, including people who have either inherited their position or been awarded it due to their contribution to society) each play an important role in the work of Parliament.

In the House of Commons, Members of Parliament (MPs) debate Bills (draft or proposed Acts of Parliament) and then vote on them to decide whether they should become laws.

Members of the House of Lords will use their experience in business, politics and/or society as a whole to consider the advantages and disadvantages of a Bill and suggest improvements.

To create a new law (Act of Parliament) a Bill is passed through both houses of Parliament: the House of Commons and the House of Lords, before gaining Royal Assent (a formality when the Queen agrees to make the Bill into an Act of Parliament).

The path of the Bill through Parliament is shown below:

For more information about how parliament works visit www.parliament.uk.

As statute law takes precedence over case law the courts cannot question the validity of an Act of Parliament.

3.3   Delegated legislation

The Government can make changes to a law without going through the process of passing an Act of Parliament if there is a provision within the original Act for **delegated legislation**.

 Definition

Delegated legislation (or secondary legislation) is law that has been passed otherwise than in an Act of Parliament. It is usually concerned with detailed changes to the law, without the need for further Acts to be passed.

For this to occur, the original Act (or primary legislation) would have had provisions that allow for future delegated legislation to alter the law to a specified extent.

The changes made under delegated legislation range in degree from technical details, for example altering the level of a fine, to filling out the substantial details of an enabling Act.

Examples of delegated legislation:

Statutory Instruments   Statutory instruments are made by government ministers who have been given powers in a parent Act to authorise detailed orders, rules or regulations. Statutory instruments are usually drafted by the legal office of the relevant government department following consultation with interested parties.

Byelaws	Byelaws are made by local authorities and only apply within a specific geographic area. They are created when there is no general legislation which deals with particular local concerns.
	They must be approved by a Secretary of State (government minister) before they can come into force.
Orders in Council	In times of emergency, the Crown and Privy Council have the power to introduce delegated legislation.

3.4 Advantages and disadvantages of delegated legislation

Advantages	Disadvantages
Saves Parliamentary time	The volume involved and lack of publicity means that it is difficult to keep up with changes introduced
Access to technical expertise leaves Parliament free to consider and debate the underlying principles	Could be challenged as being undemocratic as changes are enacted without review by the elected House of Commons
Flexibility – it is quick and easy to make and to change	

Test your understanding 2

Which of the following statements regarding delegated legislation are correct? Tick all that apply.

Statement	Correct?
Delegated legislation must be passed in Parliament the same way as direct legislation.	
Byelaws are an example of delegated legislation.	

4 Public law and private law

4.1 The differences between public law and private law

Within the English legal system, two distinct areas of law operate: private and public law. They both aim to create social order, but have a number of distinct differences.

Within public law, different categories exist. These include criminal law, constitutional law, administrative law, social welfare law and all deal with matters relating to the whole country or society as a whole.

Private law is concerned with the law enforced between individuals. This can include contract law, family law and other areas which deal with intellectual property rights (copyrights, design and patents), land law, probate (dealing with wills and how property is distributed after someone dies) and company law (which deals with the ways in which companies are created and rules regulating how they operate their business).

5 Criminal law and civil law

5.1 The differences between criminal law and civil law

In all modern societies, legal rules fall into two fundamental categories.

CRIMINAL LAW ensures that every citizen in a society knows the boundaries of acceptable conduct. Criminal offences are considered to be an offence against the whole community, and so are prosecuted in the name of the state (or specifically, the Queen).

CIVIL LAW protects individuals against one another by specifying the rights and duties of individuals. The person who takes out the lawsuit is called the **claimant**. He or she will sue the party believed to be responsible, known as the **defendant**.

Because of these differences, the two legal systems are treated differently in the court system.

KAPLAN PUBLISHING

The main differences are summarised in the following table:

	Criminal	**Civil**
Court	Magistrates Court or Crown Court	County Court or High Court
Purpose	To enforce forms of behaviour by punishing wrongdoers for offences against society	To regulate relationships between individuals by settling disputes
Commencement of Action	The case is brought by the police or Crown Prosecution Service (CPS) in the name of the Crown	The case is brought by an individual who is seeking a remedy from another individual or organisation
When a case is brought against someone, they are …	Charged with an offence; prosecuted	Sued
The accused is called…	The defendant	The defendant
The person starting the case is called…	The prosecution	The claimant
The case is referred to 'as'	R v (name of the defendant)	(defendant's name) v (claimant's name)
Burden of proof	The prosecution have to prove guilt beyond reasonable doubt (higher standard of proof)	The claimant must prove liability or fault on the balance of probabilities (lower standard of proof)
Outcome	Conviction or acquittal	Defendant is liable or not liable to the claimant
Remedy	A punishment imposed by the state, e.g. a fine or a period of imprisonment	A court order to the defendant to pay damages to the claimant, or an equitable remedy, e.g. injunction

Test your understanding 3

Which **one** of the following would be judged under civil law?

A   A prosecution for murder

B   An action by a claimant for £1 million damages for fraudulent misrepresentation

C   Proceedings where the accused is tried for the offence of applying a false trade description for goods

D   A prosecution by HMRC for non-payment of tax

5.2   The criminal and civil court system

Cases progress through the court system depending upon the seriousness of the crime or the complexity of the case.

All minor criminal matters are dealt with by the Magistrates Court. Serious cases are referred up to the Crown Court where the case is heard before a jury and presided over by a judge. Appeals are heard in the Court of Appeal (Criminal Division).

Most civil cases are heard, in the first instance, by the County Court, although if large amounts of money are involved, they will be initially held in the High Court. Appeals are held in the Court of Appeal (Civil Division).

The highest court is the Supreme Court, which considers appeals that concern points of law of general public importance.

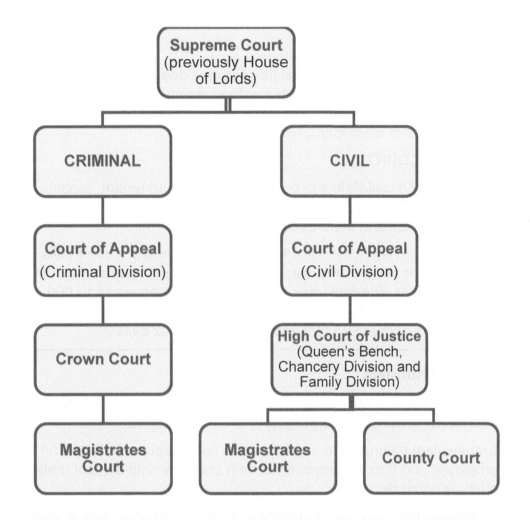

 Examples – the civil courts

SUPREME COURT

Normally it consists of five Justices of Supreme Court hearing appeals from the Court of Appeal and very occasionally from the High Court.

COURT OF APPEAL

Three Lord Justices of Appeal hear appeals from both the High Court and County Courts.

HIGH COURT OF JUSTICE

One High Court judge in the first instance, two or three for appeals.

The High Court is split into three divisions, based on the type of claims heard.

The Queen's Bench Division hears the first instance cases of contract and tort. The Chancery Division deals with land law, trusts, company law, insolvency, etc. The Family Division hears matrimonial cases.

MAGISTRATES COURT

Although it mainly has criminal jurisdiction it does have civil jurisdiction in family matters such as contact orders, maintenance and adoption. There are also powers of recovery of council tax arrears and charges for water, gas and electricity.

COUNTY COURT

First instance civil claims in contract, tort, landlord/tenant, probate and insolvency. One district judge hears small claims, one circuit judge hears most fast-track and multi-track cases.

When a claim is received it will be allocated to one of three tracks for the hearing. The small claims track is more informal and deals with claims of up to £10,000. The fast-track deals with claims between £10,000 and £25,000 expected to not last more than one day. The multi-track deals with claims of over £25,000 and/or more complex cases.

5.3   Tribunals

Tribunals are also an important part of the English legal system and are an alternative to using the court system to settle a dispute.

Employment tribunals are established to hear disputes between an employee and their employer on certain statutory employment matters, such as unfair dismissal.

Employment tribunals are composed of one employment judge, plus two expert laypeople who are drawn from panels representing both sides of the industry.

Appeals are made to the employment appeal tribunal (EAT) and can only be made on a point of law.

The EAT is composed of one High Court judge, plus two or four expert laypeople.

Court v Tribunal

	Court	Tribunal
Expertise	Case may not be heard by a specialist in that particular area of law.	Case will be heard by someone who has expertise in that area.
Speed	A slower process.	A much quicker process.
Cost	Legal aid may be available but if not can be an expensive process.	Legal aid is not available (except for land tribunals and EAT's) but can be a much cheaper procedure.
Proceedings	Strict rules relating to evidence, pleading and procedure.	Much less formal and can be less intimidating.
Decisions	Are bound by the doctrine of judicial precedent, therefore making consistent decisions.	Not bound by the doctrine of judicial precedent, therefore at risk of making inconsistent decisions.

6 Summary

This chapter has focused on how the English legal system has developed over time. You will have learnt about the sources of law: case law and statute law. In relation to case law, judicial precedent is an important principle which determines which decisions are followed in later cases.

You covered the different classifications of law, these being private law and public law as well as criminal law and civil law. The classification of criminal law and civil law is important as this then determines the court system that a case would progress through.

Test your understanding answers

Test your understanding 1

	Correct?
US Federal Law	
AAT conceptual framework	
UK common law	✓
Acts of Parliament	✓

Test your understanding 2

Statement	Correct?
Delegated legislation must be passed in Parliament the same way as direct legislation.	
Byelaws are an example of delegated legislation.	✓

Test your understanding 3

The correct answer is B.

An action by a claimant for £1 million damages for fraudulent misrepresentation should be judged under civil law.

Contract law

2

Introduction

Contract law is the branch of civil law which determines whether or not a promise is legally binding (i.e. enforceable by a court of law). Contracts form the basis of most commercial transactions and, for this reason, it is important for accounting professionals to be aware of the main elements of contract law.

ASSESSMENT CRITERIA
1.3 Key features of contracts
1.4 Remedies available for breach of contract

CONTENTS
1 Essential elements of a contract
2 Discharging a contract
3 Remedies for a breach of contract

1 Essential elements of a contract

1.1 What is a contract?

A contract is a legally enforceable agreement. Most contracts can be written, verbal or a mixture of the two. It can also be implied from the conduct of the parties. For example, all of the following everyday transactions are contracts: purchasing a newspaper; buying a bus ticket; purchasing a sandwich; buying a book or a CD.

A contract that does not required by law to be in writing is known as a **simple contract**.

Businesses enter into contracts every time they agree to sell or purchase goods and services. In this section we will look at the elements which make up a **valid contract**.

1.2 Valid contracts

 Definition

A **valid contract** is one which is legally binding. Therefore, valid contracts are those that meet all legal requirements.

To amount to a valid contract, the following essential elements **must** be present:

Agreement	The parties in the contract must be in agreement. One party makes **an offer** which is **accepted** by the other party to the contract.
Consideration	A two-sided bargain where each side provides or promises to provide something in return for what the other is providing.
Capacity	The parties must have the capacity, or ability, to contract and submit themselves to the authority of the law. For example, persons under the age of eighteen (minors) and persons of unsound mind or under the influence of alcohol, have limitations on their power to contract.
Legality	A contract is not legally enforceable if it is deemed to be illegal.

We will now consider each of these essential elements in turn.

Test your understanding 1

Which of the following are essential elements of a valid contract?

(i)   It must be in writing

(ii) The parties must be in agreement

(iii) Each party must provide consideration

A   (i) and (ii) only

B   (ii) and (iii) only

C   (i) and (iii) only

D   (i), (ii) and (iii)

1.3   Agreement

An agreement is made when an offer has been accepted.

AGREEMENT   =   **OFFER**   +   **ACCEPTANCE**

It is important to understand the legal implications of these terms:

 Definition

An offer is a definite and unequivocal statement of willingness to be bound on specified terms without further negotiations.

The offeror is the party making the offer.

The offeree is the party receiving and accepting the offer.

If you make an offer it means that you are stating that you are willing to be bound to a contract in its current form with no changes required.

An offer can be in any form – oral, written or by conduct. It is made by an offeror. However, it is not effective until it has been communicated by the person making the offer to the recipient (the offeree).

An offer can only be accepted and hence a binding contract created if it has been **communicated** to the offeree. Communication may be either express (oral or written) or implied (through conduct).

 Example

If a reward is offered for the return of a lost item, it cannot be claimed by someone who did not know of the reward before they returned the item.

An offer can be made to a specific person, to a group of people, or to the world at large.

 Example

A famous case of an offer made to the whole world is **Carlill v Carbolic Smoke Ball Company, (1893)**. The manufacturers of the medicinal 'smoke ball' claimed that anyone who bought the ball and used it as directed would not catch influenza and if they did, a reward of £100 could be claimed.

Mrs Carlill used the ball as directed and caught influenza. The manufacturers claimed that their claim was not a legal offer and even if it was, it was not possible to make an offer to the whole world, only to individuals. Likewise, they claimed that even if they could make an offer to the whole world, Mrs Carlill had not communicated her acceptance of the offer.

The court rejected these claims and stated that it was possible to make an offer to the whole world, the contract being formed with the limited number of people who accepted its terms in good faith by coming forward and buying the product. By using the smoke ball as instructed, and having purchased it under these conditions, the court ruled that Mrs Carlill's actions had expressed an acceptance.

1.4 Termination of an offer

An offer can be terminated by:

Revocation	An offer can be withdrawn by the offeror at any time before it is accepted, even if the offeror has agreed to keep the offer open for a certain period. The revocation must be communicated to the offeree, i.e. it must be brought to their actual notice. This can be done by the offeror personally or a reliable third party.
Rejection	An offeree may reject the offer outright or make a counter offer.
Lapse	An offer will lapse on: • the death of the offeror or the offeree • the expiry of a fixed time (if given) or after a reasonable time. What is a 'reasonable time' will depend on the subject matter of the transaction.

Once an offer has been terminated, it cannot be accepted.

KAPLAN PUBLISHING

1.5   Acceptance of an offer

Once an offer has been made, subject to it not being terminated, the next stage is for the offer to be **accepted**.

 Definition

Acceptance is the unqualified and unconditional agreement to all the terms of the offer.

It must be **communicated** to the offeror by word or action.

One of the key challenges in contract law is to establish when an offer has been made and, if so, when it has been accepted.

For example, imagine you are in a shop looking to buy a magazine. Who makes the offer and who accepts? Do you make the offer to buy the magazine that the shopkeeper accepts or does the shopkeeper offer to sell you the magazine that you accept?

If the shopkeeper makes the offer to sell you the magazine, when would you accept?

(i)   When you pick up the magazine to flick through?

(ii)   When you put it in your basket?

(iii)   When you walk to the counter?

(iv)   When you stand at the till?

If any of these were correct, does this mean you cannot change your mind without breaching a contract?

Fortunately, case law helps here as this question has come before the courts. The leading case is **Pharmaceutical Society of Great Britain v Boots Cash Chemists (1953)**, which concerned medicine on a counter in a shop. In this case the judge ruled that the shopkeeper accepts your offer when your payment is taken.

Logically, this must be correct. It is at this point that you are committing to buy the magazine. At every other stage, you can change your mind, turn around and returning the magazine to the rack. It would be illogical if you were entering a binding contract just by putting an item your basket.

1.6   Invitation to treat

Offers must be distinguished from other actions which may appear to be similar. An **invitation to treat** is not an offer. Displays in shops are usually classed as **invitations to treat**. They do not represent offers by the shops for the customer to accept; instead the customer makes the offer when they take the item to the till to pay. Most adverts are also classed as invitations to treat.

Definition

An **invitation to treat** is an invitation to the other party to make an offer. For example, "we may be prepared to sell Product X at Price Y".

Example

An example of an **invitation to treat** is an advertisement, price ticket in a shop or trade price list where a written order from a customer is then the **offer**.

A frequently asked question concerns what happens when a shop prices an item incorrectly in a display. Do they have to honour it at the counter? Let us say you have had your eye on a fabulous new jacket, but the price is £79.99. One day you go into the shop and the jacket has an 'up to 50% off' sticker on it. Despite the price tag showing a price of £39.99, when the cashier runs the barcode under the scanner, it shows at the original £79.99. Can you insist they sell it to you at £39.99?

In this instance, it is crucial to determine who makes the offer in a shop and who accepts. You, the consumer, make the offer. If the shop refuses to accept your offer to buy the jacket at £39.99 then there is no contract. You cannot force the shop to accept.

So how does this work with websites? Does the company accept your offer when it takes your payment? Does it happen when you click 'submit'? The difficulty for online retailers is that many of these processes, including taking payment, are often automated. What if an employee accidently puts the wrong price on the item? Must the company honour the mistake?

This has happened on several occasions. Argos famously advertised £299 televisions for £2.99 on its website, which led to one customer placing an order for 1,700 sets. Did Argos have to honour? In short, no.

Most people happily click past the terms and conditions on the way to the checkout. However, the T&C are where the retailer tells you about contract formation. It is standard now for the retailer to state at what point in the process the contract is formed.

Many retailers have changed their acceptance to when they ship your order, not when they take your money. This means if they spot the error (not difficult if somebody places an order for 1,700 items) before they ship, you cannot argue you had a contract and they are not obliged to sell to you at that price.

1.7 Counter offers

Of course, there is no obligation for every offeree to accept every offer they receive. If unhappy with the original offer, a counter offer can be made.

 Definition

A counter offer is an offer made in response to a previous offer. As seen above, making a counter offer automatically terminates the prior offer and requires an acceptance under the terms of the counter offer or there is no contract.

 Example

Jurgen is a football manager. He wants to buy a footballer from Southampton FC and he offers £60 million.

The Southampton FC manager responds that he will only accept £70 million for the player.

The Southampton FC manager has made a counter offer for the player. This has destroyed Jurgen's original offer, which cannot now be resurrected.

Jurgen says, "No thanks, that is too much for me to pay for the player".

The Southampton FC manager cannot now go back and accept the original offer of £60 million. That offer no longer exists. Jurgen is now under no obligation to pay £60 million. There is no contract.

Counter offers can go on indefinitely. You can make a counter offer to a counter offer, repeatedly until one party accepts the latest offer. The key is that each counter destroys any earlier offers. The earlier offers no legal have any legal effect.

1.8 Acceptance and "subject to contract"

Acceptance is **unconditional** agreement. This can be seen where the offeree can signal acceptance to the question "Do you accept?" by simply saying "yes". If there are other conditions attached to the acceptance (i.e. the answer is "yes, but only if…"), then it will likely be a counter offer.

Sometimes an offer is accepted on a **"subject to contract"** basis. This means that whilst an agreement has been made, there may be terms and conditions written into the contract that need to be agreed by both parties.

Therefore, the words "subject to contract" mean that the parties are not legally bound until a contract has been executed (completed). Even though both parties have agreed terms, the matter effectively remains in a state of negotiation. Furthermore, either party can withdraw from the transaction without liability.

 Example

Joseph has a sign in his car stating, 'For Sale, £1,200'. **(Invitation to treat)**

Benjamin offers £800 to Joseph. **(Offer)**

Joseph does not accept but responds to Benjamin that the lowest he would accept is £1,000. **(Counter offer)**

Benjamin accepts that price so long as the car has a valid MOT certificate. **(Counter offer)**

This is still not an agreement as Benjamin's response has a condition that must be met.

Once Joseph proves he has a valid MOT and Benjamin accepts this certificate there has been:

- An offer (to buy the car), and

- Acceptance (Joseph provides the certificate).

 Test your understanding 2

Betty is the owner of a haberdashery and put a notice in the window of her shop advertising that all the price of fabric has 20% off. This is:

A   A completed contract

B   An acceptance of an offer

C   A contractual offer

D   An invitation to treat

1.9 Consideration

Before a simple binding contract exists, both parties must have **agreed to provide something of value to the other**. This exchange is termed the consideration and converts the promises of the parties into bargains enforceable by the courts.

Example

Joseph has agreed to sell his car to Benjamin for £1,000.

Joseph will be suffering the loss of his car but gaining the benefit of £1,000.

Benjamin will be suffering the loss of £1,000 but gaining the benefit of the car.

Therefore, a valid agreement has been formed to provide something of value to each other.

Definition

Consideration can be defined as some right, interest, profit or benefit gained by one party, or some detriment, loss or responsibility given, suffered or undertaken by the other.

The consideration needs to satisfy the following criteria:

Sufficient	It must be of some value (usually monetary), even if it is a minimal value. It does not have to be adequate, i.e. represent the true value of the exchange. For example if £100 was paid for some land worth £50,000, the £100 would still be valid consideration.
Legal	The exchange should not be against the law.
Timely	Consideration must not be past i.e. something that has already been provided at the time the contract is made. It must be exchanged at the time the contract is made, or at a later date (see below).
Executed **Or** **Executory**	The consideration is carried out at the time the contract is made. For example, handing over 60p and receiving a newspaper. An exchange of promises to do something in the future. For example, when there is an agreement to pay for goods 'cash on delivery'. The payment and the delivery are 'executory' – completed at a later date.

Example

Joseph offers to sell his car to Benjamin for £1,000. Benjamin agrees to pay £1,000 for Joseph's car. There has been and offer and acceptance and consideration on both sides – a simple contract has been formed.

1.10 Capacity and legality

Each person entering into the contract must have the ability (i.e. capacity) to be able to do so. The following groups are considered to have limitations on their power to contract and would not be bound to **some** types of contracts (e.g. financial contracts such as loan agreements):

- Minors – persons under the age of 18 years old
- Persons of unsound mind
- Anyone under the influence of alcohol or drugs.

In addition, for a contract to be valid it must be for a legal purpose. For example, a contract relating to drug dealing is against the law and any disputes between the parties would not be heard in a court of law.

1.11 Types of contracts

A **void** contract is one that **cannot be enforced by law**. An agreement to carry out an illegal act or an agreement that is impossible to carry out are examples of void contracts.

A **voidable** contract is a valid contract that can be made legally null and void by one party to the contract. A contract where one party, e.g. a minor, does not have capacity is an example of a voidable contract, as the other party is bound by the contract if the minor wants to continue with it but the minor has the option of setting the contract aside.

2 Discharging a contract

2.1 Ways to end a contract

This section covers the different ways in which a contract can be brought to an end (discharged).

For the purpose of this exam, there are two ways this can be achieved:

- by performance
- by breach of contract.

2.2 Discharge by performance

A contract is usually discharged by the performance by both parties of their obligations under the contract.

The general rule is that performance must be exact and precise and that a partial performance is no performance.

 Example

Cutter v Powell (1795)

Cutter was contracted as part of a crew to sail a ship from Jamaica to the UK. He died before completing the journey. His wife tried to sue Powell to recover part of the money due to her husband.

HELD: The widow was not entitled to anything because her husband had not completed the journey and there was no complete performance of the contract.

2.3 Discharge by breach of contract

A breach of contract occurs when one of the parties to the agreement fails to comply, either completely or satisfactorily, with their obligations under it.

 Definitions

Actual breach occurs when the breach occurs on the due date for performance.

Anticipatory breach occurs when, before the due date for performance, one of the parties shows an intention not to perform their contractual obligations.

This may be:

- **express** – one of the parties declares that they have no intention of carrying out their contractual obligations, or

- **implied** – one of the parties does something which makes subsequent performance of their contractual undertaking impossible. For example, someone who has a contract to hire out a music hall in a specific location on a future date, decides to knock down the hall to build houses on the land, before the due date of the contract.

3 Remedies for a breach of contract

3.1 Types of remedies

This section examines the remedies that may be available to any injured party as a result of a breach of contract.

As we established in the previous chapter, in common law systems, remedies can be divided into two categories: legal damages and equitable remedies.

Legal damages enable the claimant to recover monetary damages. **Equitable remedies** are granted when monetary compensation is inadequate. Where there is a conflict between legal and equitable remedies, equity will prevail.

Note that not every breach has the effect of discharging the contract and releasing the innocent party from his or her obligations:

- Breach of a condition (an important term in the contract) does entitle the innocent party to withdraw from their side of the contract – as well as seek a remedy for the breach.

- Breach of a warranty (a minor term) does not entitle the innocent party to withdraw from their side of the contract – but they can still seek a remedy for the breach.

3.2 Damages

This is the basic common law remedy for a breach and takes the form of monetary compensation with the aim of putting the claimant back into the same financial position he or she would have been in if the contract had been performed properly.

The amount payable is known as the **loss of the bargain**. This will include the return of any money paid by the claimant plus any **consequential losses** incurred as a result of the breach in contract.

The test for these consequential losses is that they should have been foreseeable to a reasonable person, when the contract was formed.

Normal losses are predictable losses arising from the breach of contract. In other words, they could have been anticipated by a reasonable person as a normal consequence of the breach, before the event.

Abnormal losses are out of the ordinary and would not be anticipated as a normal consequence of the breach. Abnormal losses can only be recovered if both parties were aware that these losses would arise as a result of a breach, at the time the contract was made.

Example

Victoria Laundry (Windsor) Ltd v Newman Industries Ltd (1949)

Newman Industries Ltd contracted to sell a boiler to Victoria Laundry (Windsor) Ltd for use in the dyeing and laundry business. The defendant was aware that the boiler was to be used immediately, however the delivery of the boiler was delayed by five months.

The claimant sued for damages both for the loss of ordinary profit and for losses incurred because it missed out on a lucrative contract because of the delayed delivery.

HELD: Damages were awarded for the loss of ordinary profits (five month delay) because the defendant could reasonably foresee these **normal losses**. However, as the defendant was not aware of the lucrative contract **when the contract was formed** they could not have reasonably foreseen that a breach would cause this loss and so were not liable for these **abnormal losses**.

3.3 Liquidated damages and penalty clauses

It is possible for the parties to agree the amount of damages payable in the event of a breach before the contract is formed. However, the parties must be careful to make sure the amount is reasonable.

A penalty clause threatens disproportionate damages for breach. The amount is often very large in relation to the expected loss. A clause is therefore considered to be a penalty clause if the stated sum is extreme when compared to the maximum loss that could happen. Where the courts find the clause to be a penalty clause it will be held to be invalid and not legally enforceable.

 Example – A penalty clause?

Parking Eye Ltd v Beavis (2015)

Parking Eye Ltd managed a car park on behalf of the owners of a retail park. They had installed prominent notices that failing to comply with a two hour maximum stay would 'result in a Parking Charge of £85'.

Mr Beavis left his car at the car park for nearly three hours and received a demand for payment of £85. Mr Beavis refused to pay and argued that this fee was so high compared to the actual breach of contract that it was a penalty charge and therefore unenforceable.

This case went to the Supreme Court due to its importance and relevance for other members of the public. The Supreme Court ruled that the £85 fee was **not** a penalty charge.

The judges ruled that the high fee had two objectives:

(i)   To provide an efficient use of the available parking spaces, ensuring a flow of shoppers into the shops and preventing commuters using the spaces for long-term stays.

(ii) To generate income for Parking Eye Ltd to run the scheme.

The fact that both Parking Eye Ltd and the shop owners had a legitimate interest in the charges was key to the decision against Mr Beavis.

The Supreme Court ruled that £85 was **no higher than necessary** to achieve the objectives.

Liquidated damages are a genuine reasonable pre-estimate of the expected loss expressly stated in the contract. The amount stated is the amount of damages claimable. There should be an explanation within the contract to show how the figures were calculated. The clause is enforceable by the court.

 Example

Dunlop Pneumatic Tyre Co v New Garage and Motor Co (1915)

The claimant supplied the defendant with tyres, under a contract which imposed a minimum retail price. The contract provided that the defendant had to pay the claimant £5 for every tyre they sold in breach of the price agreement. When the defendant sold tyres at less than the agreed minimum price, they resisted the claim for £5 per tyre, on the grounds that it represented a penalty clause.

HELD: The provision was a genuine attempt to fix damages, and was not a penalty. It was, therefore, enforceable.

3.4   Equitable remedies

Equitable remedies are granted when monetary compensation through damages is not adequate.

They are only available at the discretion of the court and include the following:

Specific Performance	Requires someone to perform their contractual obligations. For example, if someone has contracted to purchase a unique item e.g. a painting, and the seller refuses to carry out the sale. This is not available for personal service contracts as the standard of performance cannot be controlled or guaranteed.
Injunction	Orders someone not to do something. For example, if land has been sold and the contract states that it should not be used for industrial purposes – and the buyer is intending to breach this term.
Rescission	Restores each of the parties to their exact pre-contractual position.

Equitable remedies are not granted if:

- damages are an adequate remedy
- the claimant has acted unfairly
- the order would cause undue hardship
- the order would require constant supervision by the court
- there is undue delay in seeking the remedy.

Example

Warner Brothers Pictures Inc v Nelson (1936)

The film star Bette Davis (Miss Nelson) entered into a contract with the claimants, whereby she agreed that she would not undertake other film work or any other occupation without the claimant's written consent.

The claimant sought an injunction to restrain her from doing film work for another company in breach of this agreement.

HELD: The injunction would be granted. However, no injunction would be granted to prevent her from engaging in 'other occupations' as this would force her to work for the claimants.

Test your understanding 3

Complete the following sentences using the pick list provided:

The remedy which requires a person to carry out his contract is known as _____. The remedy requiring a person not to act in breach of contract is known as an _____. These are both _____ remedies and, as such, are discretionary. If the contract contains a provision which is designed to intimidate the other party into completing the contract by setting down a disproportionate sum payable in the event of a breach, the provision will be regarded as a _____ clause and will be treated as _____, that is, of no legal effect.

Pick list:

specific performance   penalty   equitable   legal

injunction   valid   void   exclusion

3.5 The Consumer Rights Act 2015

The Consumer Rights Act 2015 is a statute that covers:

- what should happen when goods or digital content are faulty; and

- how services should match up to what has been agreed and what should happen when they do not.

When a product is sold it must be of satisfactory quality, fit for purpose and as described. The goods supplied must match any description given to you, or any models or samples shown to you at the time of purchase.

If goods which are purchased are faulty the following remedies are available:

- Up to thirty days – an immediate refund.

- Up to six months – the right to have the item repaired or replaced. If the attempt to repair or replace the item is unsuccessful the consumer has the right to a refund or a price reduction.

- Up to six years – if the goods do not last a reasonable length of time the consumer may be entitled to some money back.

A service must be carried out with reasonable care and skill. In practice this means that a service must be carried out to the same or similar standard to that which is considered acceptable within their trade or profession. Industry standards within a particular service sector and relevant codes of practice are useful benchmarks to consider when deciding whether a service has been carried out with reasonable care and skill.

If a service has not been provided with reasonable care and skill the following remedies are available:

- Right to repeat performance – where a service is not carried out with reasonable care and skill then the service must be performed again so that it conforms to the contract.

- Right to a price reduction – if repeat performance of a service is impossible or it cannot be carried out within a reasonable time or without causing significant inconvenience, then the consumer is entitled to a price reduction. A price reduction can be calculated by comparing the difference between the contract price and the value of the service actually performed.

4 Summary

This chapter has focused on what a contract is, in particular the essential elements that make up a contract and the various forms contracts may take.

When a contract has been formed, it's important to know the different ways in which the parties' contractual obligations can come to an end. This can be by performance of the contract or by breach of the contract. Remember there are two types of breach of contract – actual and anticipatory.

Finally, we looked at the different remedies available when there is a breach of contract. Damages are a common law remedy. There are equitable remedies available at the discretion of the court. If you buy faulty goods or receive a sub-standard service, you will be entitled to remedies under the Consumer Rights Act 2015.

Test your understanding answers

 Test your understanding 1

The correct answer is B.

A valid contract does not need to be in writing.

 Test your understanding 2

The correct answer is D.

Betty's sign showing 20% off is an invitation to treat.

 Test your understanding 3

The remedy which requires a person to carry out his contract is known as **specific performance**. The remedy requiring a person not to act in breach of contract is known as an **injunction**. These are both **equitable** remedies and, as such, are discretionary. If the contract contains a provision which is designed to intimidate the other party into completing the contract by setting down a disproportionate sum payable in the event of a breach, the provision will be regarded as a **penalty** clause and will be treated as **void**, that is, of no legal effect.

External business environment

3

Introduction

In this chapter, you will learn to appreciate the factors outside of a business that may have an impact on that organisation's present or future activities. You will understand that these factors can result from the activities of outside organisations such as other businesses and government. Often, what competitors do has an impact on how our business must change and adapt. Similarly, the policies that government implements can have a similar impact.

ASSESSMENT CRITERIA	CONTENTS
2.1 The economic environment	1 Economic environment
2.2 Government control of the economy	2 Government control of the economy
2.3 The competitive environment	3 Competitive environment

1 Economic environment

It is important in any organisation to assess the economic factors which will affect its industry. This will enable the organisation to identify potential opportunities and threats.

Economics can be defined in various ways, one of which is 'the study of how society allocates scarce resources, which have alternative uses, between competing ends'.

1.1 Microeconomic environment

It is useful to distinguish between two aspects of economics:

 Definition

Microeconomics is the study of the economic behaviour of individual consumers, firms and industries. It focuses on how these three individual parts of an economy make decisions about how to allocate scarce resources.

 Definition

Macroeconomics considers aggregate behaviour, and the sum of individual economic decisions – in other words, the workings of the economy as a whole.

Microeconomics attempts to examine supply and demand decisions made by these individuals and how these affect the selling prices of goods and services within an industry or market.

The syllabus at this level only covers microeconomics. You will cover macroeconomics in the Business Awareness paper at level 4.

1.2 Demand

Individual demand shows how much of a good or service someone intends to buy at different prices. This demand needs to be effective, in that consumers need to have the cash available to buy the goods or services. When considering the level of demand at a given price, we assume that the 'conditions of demand' (i.e. other variables) are held constant.

Demand tends to be higher at a low price and lower at a high price for most goods and services. This is the result of two processes:

- the **substitution** effect. This is where a consumer buys more of one good and less of another because of relative price changes. Thus if two goods are substitutes a fall in the price of the first will lead consumers to switch some demand to the lower-priced good, substituting the first good for the second.

- the **income** effect. This is where a change in the price of a good affects the purchasing power of the consumer's income (a change in their real income). If the price of a good falls, the consumer experiences a rise in their real income and, as a result, tends to buy more.

When the demand for a good or service changes in response to a change in its price, the change is referred to as:

- an **expansion** in demand as demand rises when the price falls.

- a **contraction** in demand as demand falls when the price rises.

 Example: Individual demand

K plc is a motor car manufacturer. It may find that if it raises the prices it sells its cars for, the demand for the vehicles, and therefore the number of cars the company sells, will fall.

This could be due to the **substitution effect**. There are a large number of car manufacturers that customers can choose between. If K raises its prices, it may become more expensive than its rivals, leading customers to switch to lower-priced alternatives offered by competitors.

K's sales may also suffer because of the **income effect**. Cars are relatively expensive, costing a high proportion of a consumer's income. If K prices its cars too high, many of its customers may simply become unable to afford the product, leading to a drop in demand.

In most cases the income effect is relatively weak. However, if expenditure on the good is a large proportion of consumer income, e.g. in the case of a house purchase, the effect will be relatively large.

The main conditions that affect demand are:

- **Income**

    Changes in income often affect demand.

    For example, lower direct taxes would raise disposable incomes making consumers better off and able to spend more on discretionary expenditure. For goods, an increase in income leads to an increase in demand. Examples include cars, jewellery, fashion clothing and music streaming services.

    For inferior goods, however, a rise in income leads to a **lower** demand for the product as consumers, now being richer, substitute better quality and preferred goods and services for the original ('inferior') good or service. An example of this is public transport. Here, as incomes rise, the demand for public transport falls as consumers substitute more expensive, private transport such as cars.

- **Tastes**

    Tastes, in particular fashions, change frequently and this may make the demand for certain goods volatile.

    A good example of this is the rapid rise in demand for fidget spinners seen in 2017 followed by a decline as people's attention moved elsewhere.

    Tastes can be manipulated through the use of advertising to 'create' markets. For example, this happened with air purifiers, a product which our ancestors survived perfectly well without. Some goods are in seasonal demand (e.g. cooked meat) even though they are available all year round, because tastes change throughout the year (e.g. more salads are consumed in the summer).

- **The price of other goods**

    If goods are in joint demand, for example, complements such as burgers and burger buns, a change in the price of one will also affect the other. Therefore, if the price of burgers falls, there is likely to be an increase in demand for burger buns.

    Where goods are substitutes (e.g. Coke and Pepsi, or McDonald's and Burger King), a rise in the price of one will cause an increase in demand for the other.

    Sometimes, technological breakthroughs result in new products coming into the market. For example, the introduction of affordable electric vehicles with extended range is reducing demand for petrol and diesel powered vehicles.

- **Population**

  An increase in population creates a larger market for most goods, thereby increasing demand. For example, an influx of seasonal workers from other countries will raise the demand for most essential goods during the season in which they are working. Changes in population distribution will also affect demand patterns. If the proportion of old people relative to young people increases, then the demand for products such as mobility aids will increase relative to that of children's toys.

 Test your understanding 1

What do you think determines the demand for hot chocolate?

1.3   Supply

Supply reflects how many units producers would be willing to offer for sale, at different prices, over a given period of time.

The supply of a business is underpinned by the desire to make profit. It demonstrates what a firm will deliver to the market at different prices.

If the price that goods can be sold at increases, each unit sold will make more profit for the supplier, meaning that they will wish to supply more units for the market.

As well as changes in price (described above), changes in costs will influence supply:

A decrease in supply

At existing sales prices, **less** will be supplied when the cost of supply increases – this is because increased costs reduce the profit made.

This may result from:

- **Higher production costs**. The costs of production may increase because the factors of production become more expensive. Conditions such as higher wage costs per unit, higher input prices and increased interest rates will lead to reductions in supply.

- **Indirect taxes**. Assuming that the total price charged to customers is unchanged the imposition of an indirect tax, such as VAT, makes supply at existing prices less profitable. With an indirect tax, the costs of production are raised directly because the tax must be deducted and paid to the tax authorities on each item sold – hence the profit margin is reduced.

An increase in supply

An increase in supply arises when the cost of production falls – this is because a reduction in costs increases the profit made.

Lower product costs may arise from:

- technological innovations, for example, the advance of microchip technology lowered the cost of computers and led to large increases in supply

- more efficient use of existing factors of production (land, labour, capital funding and entrepreneurship). For example, introduction of a shift system of working might mean fuller use of productive capacity, leading to lower unit costs

- improvements in productivity that allow maintenance of output levels with fewer workers

- lower input prices, such as cheaper raw material imports and lower-priced components bringing down production costs

- a reduction or abolition of an indirect tax or the application of, or increase in subsidies.

1.4   Profit motive

What is the primary purpose of a business? Ultimately, it's to make a profit. This is achieved by selling a product or service at a market price that is higher than the production cost. This desire is known as the **profit motive** of a business.

There are many considerations when a business starts to produce a good or service:

- how to make production efficient?

- what premises are necessary to run the business?

- what are the staffing needs of the business?

- what is the selling price of the product or service?

When making decisions such as these the profit motive is a guiding factor.

A business has to balance the profit motive with risks and uncertainty. All businesses face risks and uncertainties, particularly new businesses.

To start a business, an entrepreneur needs money to put into the business to buy supplies and pay wages. Often the entrepreneur will use their own money as well as borrowing from a bank. They may even borrow money from friends and family. However, if the business doesn't make enough profit to pay back all the money that's been borrowed, it will fail and potentially some or all of the money that was invested in the business will be lost.

1.5 Globalisation

Globalisation is the process by which businesses and countries around the world become more connected. It has resulted in single businesses operating in lots of countries. They can be based anywhere, and can buy from and sell to any country.

Technological advances such as the internet and mobile phones have speeded up communications to the extent that financial transactions can be carried out instantaneously, whilst improvements in supply chains and logistics mean that goods can be shipped relatively cheaply and quickly in the world.

Developments in manufacturing techniques have meant that economies of scale are being utilised in many industries. This is driving down costs and therefore attracting overseas buyers.

Competition also fuels globalisation. After all, if your competitor decides to gain a competitive advantage by globalising would you want to be left behind? If you want to compete you will probably follow suit.

We'll consider the advantages and disadvantages of globalisation later on in this chapter.

2 Government control of the economy

Definition

An economy of a country is a collection of business transactions that take place throughout the country, throughout the year.

In practice the economy represents lots of businesses buying and selling with each other, selling directly to domestic and international customers, as well as the money spent by government.

What role does the government have in the economy?

2.1 Key objective

A key objective for any government is to maintain a **steady economy**.

A change in the economy could be good or bad for business. For instance, a slow-down in the economy may lead to rising unemployment. If people are out of work they cut back their spending, especially on luxuries. This may lead to a sharp decline in sales at restaurants, jewellers and more expensive shops.

Many businesses start up when times are good when it seems easy to make money from free-spending customers. However, it is important to remember that hard times may be around the corner in the form of a recession.

So how do we measure the state of an economy?

Firstly, we look at the rate of **unemployment**. Unemployment is when someone of working age wants a job but cannot get one. The level of unemployment is closely associated with the overall state of the economy. During the recessions of the early 1990s and 2009–10 in the UK, unemployment became a serious problem, especially for younger people. More than 20% of 18 to 24 year olds were unemployed in the UK in 2012 and 2013. The impact of unemployment on different businesses varies considerably. Producers of essentials such as toilet paper and soap will suffer little effect from economic highs or lows – people have little choice to buy such essentials. However, those producing luxury goods are more susceptible to an economic downturn, perhaps resulting in staff redundancies.

Another measure is the rate of **inflation**. Inflation represents the general rate of price increases over a period, i.e. it measures how much prices are rising in percentage terms. The 'rate of inflation' means the percentage change in prices compared with a year ago. When inflation is low (the bank of England inflation target is 2%) businesses can easily cope with increases in input costs such as materials. But if prices are rising more sharply, not only do costs increase but these increases may have to be passed on to customers by increasing sales prices, in order to continue selling goods or services at a profit. Of course increasing prices may result in a negative reaction by customers and reduced demand. Deflation is the opposite to inflation and occurs when inflation falls to below 0%. This results in customers paying less for goods and services.

Gross domestic product (GDP) is also a measure of how well an economy is performing. GDP measures the monetary value of final goods and services that are bought by the final user that are produced in a country in a given period of time (say a quarter or a year). It counts all of the output generated within the borders of a country. In broad terms, an increase in real GDP is interpreted as a sign that the economy is doing well.

2.2 Government influence

There are a number of ways in which a government can influence the economy.

Government spending can be a useful tool in boosting the economy.

 Definition

Fiscal policy is the use of government spending and/or taxation as a tool to influence the economy.

Fiscal policy can be expansionary or contractionary. An expansionary fiscal policy is an increase in government spending (or decrease in tax) in order to stimulate the economy. This can be used by governments during a recession. An increase in government spending directly increases demand for goods and services, which can help increase output and employment. A contractionary policy, on the other hand, has the opposite effect. It can be used by governments to cool the economy down during an economic boom.

The way the government chooses to tax businesses and individuals will also have an effect.

Different types of business (e.g. companies or sole traders) are also taxed differently (covered in more detail in chapter 5).

The other impact on business comes from the way that the government taxes individuals and goods. Individuals are subject to income tax on their income and they pay VAT on goods and services. Broadly, the higher the rate of tax, the harder it is for households to spend and, therefore, the worse it is for businesses.

Government can also implement legislation which can result in extra costs to a business. New laws can represent opportunities or threats to businesses. Let's use the National Minimum Wage as an example. This means that employers have to pay their staff a minimum amount. The exact amount depends on the age of the worker and the type of work. On one hand this increases costs for businesses which can lead to increased prices. On the other hand this can lead to better motivated staff and increased productivity. Another positive effect is that as workers are paid more they have greater spending power which drives demand for products.

Test your understanding 2

(a) What is the effect on the economy if there is an increase in government spending?

(b) What is the effect on the economy if there is an increase in tax?

2.3 Effective tax system

Governments need tax revenues to finance expenditure on public services such as hospitals, schools, policing, retirement pensions, social benefits and to finance government borrowing. Governments can use tax to stimulate one sector of the economy and control another. For example, certain tax advantages on capital expenditure may develop the manufacturing sector, while high taxes on tobacco and alcohol may discourage sales.

In **Wealth of Nations**, Adam Smith proposed that a good tax should have the following characteristics:

- fair (reflect a person's ability to pay)

- absolute (certain not arbitrary)

- convenient (easy to pay)

- efficient (low collection costs)

The 3 major principles of good tax policy are as follows:

- Equity – a good tax should be fairly levied between one taxpayer and another.

- Efficiency – a good tax should be cheap and easy to collect for the government, i.e. the UK tax system uses PAYE (pay-as-you-earn) to collect tax at source on salaries and wages.

- Economic effects – a good tax should reflect the individual's ability to pay. Economic effect states that the amount of tax an individual pays should be dependent on the level of burden the tax will create relative to the wealth of the individual.

There are three types of taxes:

- Progressive taxes: These take an increasing proportion of income as income rises; for example, UK income tax has higher rates of tax for higher levels of income. A progressive tax takes a higher percentage of tax from people with higher incomes. It means that the more a person earns, the higher their average rate of tax will be.

- Proportional taxes: These take the same proportion of income as income rises. In other words, the same rate of tax is paid regardless of income.

- Regressive taxes: These take a decreasing proportion of income as income rises. A regressive tax is a tax which takes a higher percentage of tax revenue from those on low incomes. This is a tax which hits the poor hardest.

The UK tax system, administered by HM Revenue and Customs (HMRC) comprises a number of different taxes. These are collected by:

- imposing taxes on individuals (direct taxes)

- imposing taxes on businesses (direct taxes)

- indirect taxes such as value added tax (VAT)

Individuals are subject to a range of taxes. They will pay income tax and national insurance contributions on their income. If they are employed this will be through the PAYE system whereby the employer will make the required deductions from their gross income and pay this over to the HMRC on their behalf. If an individual sells a capital asset and makes a profit they will be subject to capital gains tax on the sale. When an individual dies, the estate that they leave behind, which is essentially their assets, will be subject to inheritance tax.

A business is also taxed in a number of ways. If it is a company it will be subject to corporation tax. Otherwise, a sole trader or partner will pay income tax through the self-assessment system. Any business that employs people will have to pay national insurance contributions. In effect, this is an extra cost for having employees.

Indirect taxes are collected from the taxpayer via an intermediary such as a retail shop. The intermediary then pays over the tax collected to HMRC. An example of indirect tax is Value Added Tax (VAT). When you buy goods or services as a consumer you pay VAT to the supplier, who then pays it over to HMRC.

2.4   Interest rates

In the UK the base interest rate is set by the Bank of England. An interest rate determines the level of interest that is paid by someone who borrows money and the level of interest they receive if they save money.

The Bank of England can change the base interest rate in order to influence inflation, normally to keep it low and stable.

A change in the base interest rate can have huge repercussions for consumer spending. For example, an increase in interest rates may encourage people not to spend if they are paying a higher rate of interest on their mortgage. Likewise, people may prefer to save rather than spend in order to benefit from higher rates of interest on their capital.

Alternatively, a decrease in interest rates may result in higher spending as people with mortgages have more disposable income due to paying less interest. Likewise, those with savings may prefer to spend their savings if the interest earned is low.

If consumers are spending more this will generate more growth in the economy which in turn will result in higher employment. However, excessive demand can push prices up (i.e. inflation).

2.5 Tariffs

 Definition

A **tariff** is a tax that the government charges on imported goods and services.

The government can use a tariff to influence the price of imports. The effect is to make the cost of goods and services from abroad more expensive to buy for businesses and individuals. This will have the knock on effect of reducing demand for imports and thereby encourage demand for home-grown substitutes. It is also a method or raising revenue for the government.

3 Competitive environment

Competition is often the biggest challenge for a business, particularly a new business. Often the environment within which a business is operating creates competition.

3.1 Globalisation

As established earlier, globalisation is the process by which businesses and countries around the world become more connected.

However, having a global market means there can be a lot more competition on all different levels. It's important for any business to differentiate themselves from the competition. There are many different ways this can be done, such as higher quality goods or unique selling points.

Globalisation has advantages and disadvantages.

One of the big advantages is that globalisation creates jobs, both domestically and abroad. Globalisation can also result in lower prices for the consumer. There will be improved access to technology and improved productivity.

In terms of disadvantages, globalisation is said to create inequality, particularly between countries. The carbon footprint of transporting goods long distances is detrimental to the environment.

3.2 Exchange rates

An important consideration when trading internationally is the exchange rate. The exchange rate tells us how currencies compare and also the price at which one currency can be traded for another.

If a country wants to import products, they'll pay for the products in the currency of the country it was made in. For example, if a British business is importing goods from the USA, they will pay for those goods in US dollars.

A country's exchange rate can be affected by that particular country's economy as well as the global economy.

If the value of the pound sterling (£) decreases **(depreciation)**, this means that businesses will be able to buy fewer dollars for the same amount of sterling (£). If a business buys products from overseas, this will result in a higher cost for them as those products will now be more expensive in sterling (£) terms.

If the value of the pound sterling (£) increases **(appreciation)**, this means that it will become more expensive for businesses abroad to buy products from the UK. This in turn will lead to less demand for those products, causing a decrease in exports.

 Test your understanding 3

You're planning on going on holiday to Turkey. The value of the pound sterling has increased against the Turkish Lira.

Explain how this will impact on the cost of buying goods and services when you are there.

4 Summary

We've looked at the many external factors that can affect a business or organisation. The economic environment can have an impact on how a business sets its prices for consumers. How much a business can supply whilst still making a profit can also have an impact. Ultimately, a business will want to make a healthy profit.

The government can also have an influence on businesses by increasing or reducing spending, changing fiscal policy or introducing new legislation.

Test your understanding answers

 Test your understanding 1

You should have come up with several factors. All of the following are likely to be relevant:

- the price of hot chocolate as the higher the price the less will be demanded.

- the price of substitutes such as other hot drinks.

- the price of complementary goods such as biscuits.

- the level of income as the more people earn the more they will be able to spend.

- external factors e.g. if the weather is cold, demand for hot chocolate is likely to increase.

 Test your understanding 2

(a) If government spending is increased, there will be an increase of cash in the economy. This will cause an increase in demand for goods and services which will result in greater expenditure in the economy.

(b) If tax is increased this will have the opposite effect. There will be a decrease in demand as people will have less money to spend which will result in less expenditure in the economy.

 Test your understanding 3

An appreciation of the pound sterling against the Turkish Lira means that you will be able to purchase more Turkish Lira for a pound. This will result in the pound sterling cost of goods and services you buy in Turkey being cheaper.

CSR, ethics and sustainability

Introduction

You should be able to identify, explain and apply in business situations, the fundamental ethical principles. In addition, you should be able to identify potential conflicts of interest and the requirement, in particular, to maintain confidentiality.

You should also be able to explain sustainability, and consider the types of policies and procedures that could be adopted by businesses in order to support sustainability.

ASSESSMENT CRITERIA	CONTENTS
3.1 Corporate social responsibilities of a business	1 Ethics – the principles
	2 Threats to principles (conflicts of interest)
3.2 Sustainability and the environment	3 AAT disciplinary process
3.3 The fundamental principles of ethics for accounting technicians	4 Sustainability and corporate social responsibility (CSR)
3.4 The need to act ethically	

1 Ethics – the principles

In the UK we have a principles-based approach rather than a rules-based approach.

1.1 Fundamental principles

If people are provided with a set of rules to follow they will apply them but may try to find loopholes, e.g. if the rules state that a gift of over £5 cannot be accepted as it may be regarded as a bribe, then 10 gifts of £4.50 may be given instead of one gift of £45, in order to get around the rule.

Alternatively, if you establish a principle not to accept gifts that may be regarded as a bribe then people should comply with the principle. They cannot state that they accepted a gift of £45 simply because 'it was within the rules'. Judgement will need to be exercised before a gift of any value is accepted to ensure acceptance is in keeping with the ethical **principles**.

The idea behind the principles-based approach is that rather than having to comply with a given set of rules, we should instead learn to act appropriately in a manner consistent with the principles.

The fundamental ethical principles you need to learn and understand are as follows:

- confidentiality
- objectivity
- professional competence and due care
- integrity
- professional behaviour.

1.2 Confidentiality

You must respect the confidentiality of information acquired as a result of professional and business relationships, and not disclose any such information to third parties without proper and specific authority, unless there is a legal or professional right or duty to disclose.

Confidential information acquired as a result of professional and business relationships should not be used for the personal advantage of you or any third parties.

In your working life you are likely to deal with a broad range of information which should remain confidential between you and those to whom the information belongs or from whom it originates. Put simply, you must ensure that you do not share any privileged information with anyone who does not have the right to receive or know such information.

This includes, but is not limited to, details of contracts, sales and purchases transactions with customers and suppliers as well as any details pertaining to employees, such as personal addresses, telephone numbers, salary or contract agreements.

The need to maintain confidentiality and protect the details of those who have dealings with your company is enshrined in law (The Data Protection Act). The Data Protection Act is the UK's implementation of the General Data Protection Regulation (GDPR).

Failure to maintain confidentiality could lead to prosecution and fines for any organisation that breaches the requirements of the Act.

1.3 Objectivity

You should not allow bias, conflict of interest or the undue influence of others to override your professional or business judgements. For example, any work you undertake should be fairly stated and presented, so that it can be relied upon by others.

1.4 Professional competence and due care

You have a professional duty to maintain your professional knowledge and skills at the level required to ensure that you are able to provide a competent service based on current developments in practice and legislation. For example, you must have technical competence for the work that you undertake. This may be obtained through a combination of professional qualifications, practical experience, or working under the supervision of another to gain experience.

You should act diligently and in accordance with applicable technical and professional standards. This means that you should not be negligent or careless in the performance of your work. If necessary, you should seek guidance from an appropriate colleague or supervisor to ensure that you perform to the necessary standard.

1.5 Integrity

You should be straightforward and honest in the performance of your work duties and responsibilities.

1.6 Professional behaviour

You should comply with relevant laws and regulations and avoid any action that could bring you or your profession into disrepute. You should behave in a manner that would be expected from a professional person carrying out their work duties and responsibilities.

 Test your understanding 1

While at a party recently, you met a client of yours who is clearly very concerned about some VAT issues. Your daily work consists of some VAT related work but you have no expertise in the specific area that your client is asking for advice on.

Which fundamental principle would be breached if you gave advice? What would the appropriate course of action be?

2 Threats to principles (conflicts of interest)

2.1 Types of threats

There are a number of threats that may affect our ability to adhere to the ethical principles. In particular, the principle of objectivity is subject to several threats, any one of which has the capacity to create a conflict of interest for you:

Self-interest– A threat to objectivity may derive from a financial or other self-interest. This could arise, for example, from a direct or indirect interest in a customer, supplier or client (such as a shareholding), or from fear of having your employment terminated as a consequence of undue commercial pressure from within or outside of the organisation.

Self-review – There may be a threat to objectivity if the work of an individual or organisation needs to be reconsidered at a later date. For example, if you are asked to recheck information that you originally prepared you may have an incentive to hide or disguise errors in order to avoid criticism.

Advocacy – An advocate acts as a representative for an individual or organisation – they are not impartial and hence cannot be considered to be objective. For example, a lawyer acting for a client is not expected to present a balanced view, but rather to represent that client's position.

Familiarity – A threat that you may become influenced by any one of a number of factors, such as:

- prior knowledge of the issue, so that you do not retain objectivity

- any relationship with your customer, supplier or employer, including personal relationships with individuals

- undue reliance upon the judgement of ethical standards of a customer, supplier, client or colleague to the extent that you become too trusting.

Intimidation – The possibility that you may become intimidated by threat, by a dominating personality or by other pressures, actual or feared. This could lead to you behaving in a manner that is not in the best interests of your employer or client. For example, a customer may threaten to buy from a competitor unless they are allowed a discount to which they are not entitled based upon the agreed terms of business between you. In the worst case scenario, it could lead to you breaking the law (for example, paying bribes).

If you believe that you are in a position where a conflict of interest could arise, it is important that you communicate this to a supervisor or manager in your organisation at the earliest opportunity. This will enable others to take appropriate action to avoid or minimise the threat.

If a conflict of interest has already arisen, it is important that you take the same action, i.e. report the matter to the most appropriate person within your organisation immediately.

You may also be able to minimise the potential for conflict of interest by, for example, immediately referring friends or family to a work colleague if they approach you for assistance – this would mean that you would not be involved in any way with any transactions or activities they entered into with your organisation.

Test your understanding 2

Review each of the practical situations below, and match each situation with the ethical principle from the drop-down menu choices that relate to it. You may use an ethical principle more than once.

	Practical situation	Ethical principle
1	A family member has advised you that they will purchase goods from the organisation you work for only if you obtain a discounted price for them. You are unsure whether or not to try to arrange this.	
2	You have been asked by your manager to calculate depreciation on motor vehicles for the year, and then to reduce the calculated amount by 10% to reduce the expense and increase profit for the year.	
3	Your supervisor has asked that you resolve any payroll queries from other employees that arise during the week ahead, in the absence of the payroll clerk. Whilst you are willing to help, you have no experience of dealing with accounting for payroll or dealing with payroll queries from other employees.	
4	A friend has asked you to disclose salary details of a mutual friend who also works with you as they believe the friend is living beyond their means and wants to try to help them if possible.	
5	A work colleague arrived late on the first day of a course and didn't bother to apologise to the course leader, and nor did they engage in the course activities during the day, explaining to you, "It's not really important and it's better than being in work for the day".	

| 6 | You are reconciling the receivables ledger control account balance with the total of the receivables ledger account balances as at 30 June 20X5 and are having problems agreeing the totals. You have experience of preparing this reconciliation on numerous occasions, and any previous problems have related to discounts allowed not being included in the relevant receivables ledger accounts. As it is nearly the end of the working day and your manager needs the completed reconciliation before you finish work, you intend to pass the reconciliation to your manager which includes the statement "reconciliation complete, except for inclusion of discounts allowed in receivables ledger accounts," without actually confirming that is the case. | |

Drop-down menu choices:

- Competence and due care
- Integrity
- Professional behaviour
- Objectivity
- Confidentiality

2.2 Safeguards

 Definition

Safeguards may eliminate or reduce such threats to an acceptable level.

They fall into two broad categories:

(i) safeguards created by the profession, legislation or regulation and

(ii) safeguards in the work environment.

Safeguards created by the profession, legislation or regulation include, but are not restricted to:

(i) educational, training and experience requirements for entry into the profession

(ii)   continuing professional development requirements

(iii) corporate governance regulations

(iv) professional standards

(v)   professional or regulatory monitoring and disciplinary procedures

(vi) external review of the reports, returns, communications or information produced by a member and carried out by a legally empowered third party.

Safeguards in the work environment include, but are not restricted to:

(i)   the employing organisation's systems of corporate oversight or other oversight structures

(ii)   the employing organisation's ethics and conduct programmes

(iii) recruitment procedures in the employing organisation emphasising the importance of employing high calibre competent staff

(iv) strong internal controls

(v)   appropriate disciplinary processes

(vi) leadership that stresses the importance of ethical behaviour and the expectation that employees will act in an ethical manner

(vii) policies and procedures to implement and monitor the quality of employee performance

(viii) timely communication of the employing organisation's policies and procedures, including any changes to them, to all employees and appropriate training and education on such policies and procedures

(ix) policies and procedures to empower and encourage employees to communicate to senior levels within the employing organisation any ethical issues that concern them without fear of retribution

(x)   consultation with another appropriate professional.

The nature of the safeguards to be applied will vary depending on the circumstances. In exercising professional judgement, a member should consider what a reasonable and informed third party, having knowledge of all relevant information, including the significance of the threat and the safeguards applied, would conclude to be unacceptable.

3 AAT disciplinary process

3.1 Grounds for disciplinary action

It shall be a ground for disciplinary action if a member is guilty of misconduct.

Definition

Misconduct can be defined as a member having conducted him/herself in such a manner as would, in the opinion of the Association, prejudice his/her status as a member or reflect adversely on the reputation of the Association; or having acted in serious or repeated breach of the Articles or of any rules, regulations or byelaws.

Example 1 – Misconduct

The following shall be conclusive proof of misconduct:

- A member has, before a court of competent jurisdiction, pleaded guilty to or has been found guilty of an indictable (serious) offence.

- A member has, in the absence of exceptional mitigating circumstances, become bankrupt or has entered into any formal arrangement with his/her creditors.

- A member has not complied with the Association's policy on continuing professional development (CPD).

- A member has unreasonably refused to cooperate with an investigation carried out in accordance with these Regulations.

- A member in practice has failed to renew his/her practicing licence before the date of expiry.

- A member has repeatedly failed to reply to correspondence from the Association.

3.2 Disciplinary action

Any one or more of the following actions may be recommended by the Investigations Team as is considered appropriate having regard to the nature and seriousness of the misconduct, the member's character and past record and to any other relevant circumstances.

In the case of a full or fellow member (but not an affiliate or student member) that he or she:

- Be expelled from the Association
- Have his/her membership of the Association suspended
- Have his/her practising licence withdrawn
- Be declared ineligible for a practising licence
- Have his/her fellow member status removed (if applicable)
- Be reprimanded or severely reprimanded
- Be fined, subject to a maximum level
- Give a written undertaking to refrain from continuing or repeating the misconduct in question.

In the case of an affiliate or student member (but not a full or fellow member) that he or she:

- Be declared unfit to become a full member
- Have his/her registration as a student withdrawn
- Be reprimanded or severely reprimanded
- Be fined, subject to a maximum level
- Be debarred from sitting the association's assessments for such period as shall be determined
- Have a relevant assessment result declared null and void
- Give a written undertaking to refrain from continuing or repeating the misconduct in question.

4 Sustainability and corporate social responsibility (CSR)

Sustainability is about meeting the needs of the present without compromising the ability of future generations to meet their own needs.

It is the practice of doing business in a way that balances economic, environmental and social needs, and as such is often referred to as **'The Three P's' – People, Planet, Profit**.

Corporate social responsibility (CSR) is a business approach that contributes to sustainable development by delivering economic, social and environmental benefits for all stakeholders.

As a result, many companies now consider how their operations affect the environment and future generations.

Examples include:

- introduction of a paper recycling policy within an office building.

- adoption of 'paperless' office procedures.

- reduction of business-related travel, perhaps by use of 'virtual' meetings, via Zoom or other telecommunication tools.

- introduction of schemes to encourage employees to use public transport, cycle, or even walk to work – such as a 'bike to work' scheme whereby a bicycle can be hired or purchased from the company at a low rate and space is provided for it to be kept at work during the day.

- introduction of energy saving schemes – whereby lights and heating are turned off when not required.

- choosing to deal only with suppliers that have similar CSR values.

This list is not exhaustive and you may well be able to think of other methods by which firms can operate in a more sustainable way.

Sustainability may well be costly at the outset when implementing CSR policies, and indeed it was originally considered to represent an additional cost to a business overall. This may explain why some organisations choose not to adopt CSR policies.

However, over time, and as the values of society itself have changed, many organisations recognise that they can reap benefits by following a sustainable path. This includes the recognition, by customers and potential customers, of the stance they are taking in trying to 'do the right thing'. This is now acknowledged by many to be a key driver to increase sales and business activity over time.

For instance, an organisation may decide to use only recyclable packaging from now on. There will clearly be a cost to the organisation to source new packaging supplies and, perhaps, pay more for their packaging. However, this should be offset by the positive effect their actions will have on the environment, and the resulting improved image that they can project to their customers and potential customers, who may well switch from a competitor.

Furthermore, with advances in technology, sustainable alternatives may save money over time through cost savings. For example, the use of solar photovoltaic panels, battery storage systems and heat pumps will reduce the cost of electricity.

5 Summary

In this chapter we have seen the importance of maintaining confidentiality of information, behaving professionally within the finance function, acting with honesty and ensuring we have up-to-date professional knowledge to perform our job role.

The importance of corporate social responsibility in the workplace has also been reviewed and ensuring that we balance the three pillars of sustainability.

Test your understanding answers

 Test your understanding 1

If you attempt to give advice on technical areas that you are not comfortable with, this will be a breach of the fundamental principle of professional competence and due care.

You should make the client aware of this and not provide any advice as this may be relied upon by the client. The most appropriate course of action would be to make an appointment with the client to discuss the matter properly after you have done some research into these specific areas, or refer them to a colleague with experience in this area.

Test your understanding 2

	Practical situation	Ethical principle
1	A family member has advised you that they will purchase goods from the organisation you work for only if you obtain a discounted price for them. You are unsure whether or not to try to arrange this.	Objectivity
2	You have been asked by your manager to calculate depreciation on motor vehicles for the year, and then to reduce the calculated amount by 10% to reduce the expense and increase profit for the year.	Integrity
3	Your supervisor has asked that you resolve any payroll queries from other employees that arise during the week ahead, in the absence of the payroll clerk. Whilst you are willing to help, you have no experience of dealing with accounting for payroll or dealing with payroll queries from other employees.	Competence and due care – specifically competence

4	A friend has asked you to disclose salary details of a mutual friend who also works with you as they believe the friend is living beyond their means and wants to try to help them if possible.	Confidentiality
5	A work colleague arrived late on the first day of a course and didn't bother to apologise to the course leader, and nor did they engage in the course activities during the day, explaining to you, "It's not really important and it's better than being in work for the day".	Professional behaviour
6	You are reconciling the receivables ledger control account balance with the total of the receivables ledger account balances as at 30 June 20X5 and are having problems agreeing the totals. You have experience of preparing this reconciliation on numerous occasions, and any previous problems have related to discounts allowed not being included in the relevant receivables ledger accounts. As it is nearly the end of the working day and your manager needs the completed reconciliation before you finish work, you intend to pass the reconciliation to your manager which includes the statement "reconciliation complete, except for inclusion of discounts allowed in receivables ledger accounts," without actually confirming that is that case.	Competence and due care – specifically due care

Different types of business entity

5

Introduction

When the decision has been made to start a business an important consideration will be which type of business entity to use.

There are many considerations such as the formation process and tax implications. It's important that a business owner is aware of these implications when making a decision.

ASSESSMENT CRITERIA
4.1 Models of business ownership
4.2 The legal administration of a business
4.3 Business formation

CONTENTS
1 Models of business ownership
2 Legal administration
3 Business formation

1 Models of business ownership

1.1 The entity concept

When a business is formed it will enter into a range of business transactions. Transactions related to a business must be recorded separately from those of its owners and any other business.

When recording transactions in a business we take into account only those events that affect that particular business.

As discussed in chapter 3, business owners have a profit motive, which is the desire to make a profit. This is often the reason why people start a business.

1.2 Profit making business entities

Definition

A **sole trader** is a business owned and operated by one person.

Definition

A **partnership** is a business owned and operated by two or more people.

Definition

A **company** is a business owned by any number of shareholders and operated by directors (who may or may not also be shareholders).

A sole trader is:

- the simplest form of business

- owned and managed by one person (although there might be any number of employees)

- fully and personally liable for any losses that the business might make.

A partnership is:

- a business owned jointly by a number of partners
- each partner is jointly and severally liable for any losses that the business might incur.

Companies are more complex and have the following characteristics:

- owned by **shareholders** (also known as members)
- there can be any number of shareholders
- shareholders elect the **directors** to run the business
- almost all companies have **limited liability**
- this means that the shareholders will not be personally liable for any losses that the company incurs
- the company is a completely separate legal entity from its owners, the shareholders.

 Test your understanding 1

Which of the following is **not** an example of a business organisation?

A   A sole trader

B   An employee

C   A company

1.3   Non-profit making entities

Not all businesses are profit-making. Some are created for other purposes.

The following are examples of non-profit making entities:

- charities
- clubs and societies
- government (or public sector) organisations.

1.4   Ownership v management and control

A business does not necessarily have to be owned and controlled by the same person or group of people.

As sole traders tend to be small businesses they are generally owned and managed by the same person. However, a sole trader can employ others to assist with the activities and management of the business. The same principle applies to partnerships.

Companies can be larger business entities and in law are recognised as a separate legal entity. As mentioned above, the owners of a company are the shareholders. A company will be managed by its directors who will manage the company's business activities. There are various rules under the Companies Act 2006 which specify the duties and responsibilities that directors have to the company.

1.5 Tax implications

The type of business entity will determine what taxes are applicable to that entity.

A company will be subject to corporation tax on its profits. It will also suffer VAT on its purchases and may charge VAT on its sales, depending upon the nature of its activities. It will also have to pay employer's national insurance contributions for any employees it has.

A partnership means the individual partners are assessed on their share of the profits. They will pay income tax and national insurance contributions on these profits. As noted above the partnership will also be liable for VAT on sales and employer's national insurance contributions for employees within the business.

A sole trader will be assessed on the profits the business makes. A sole trader will pay income tax and national insurance contributions on the profits, just like a partner. Again, the sole trader will also be liable for VAT on sales and employer's national insurance contributions for employees within the business.

1.6 Limited liability

One of the key consequences of a business entity being a company is that its shareholders have limited liability. This means that, in the event that the business fails, the shareholders will only be asked to contribute identifiable amounts to the assets of the business. The company itself remains fully liable for its debts.

Sole traders and partnerships do not have limited liability. A sole trader or partners in a partnership are fully liable for the debts of the business.

2 Legal administration

The legal administration required will differ depending on whether the business entity is a sole trader or a company.

2.1 Sole trader

One of the advantages of being a sole trader is that there are no formal requirements to submit accounts to any public registry or body.

However, a sole trader does need to pay income tax on the business profits. For this purpose the sole trader will need to maintain records of business income and expenses.

These include details of:

- sales and income
- expenses
- VAT paid and charged (if VAT registered)
- PAYE deducted from employee's salaries

These records must be kept for five years from the deadline for the submission of the tax return for the period to which they relate.

2.2 Company

In contrast, a company has several legal requirements.

They have to maintain the following **statutory registers**:

- members
- directors and company secretary
- charges
- persons with significant control

The registers must be kept at the company's registered office and be available for public inspection.

The following are also required:

Confirmation statement	Can be sent at any time but no more than 12 months can pass between each statement.
	The statement confirms that no changes to key information have happened during the year. If changes have been made it states what they are.
	Changes need to be communicated on:
	• address of registered office
	• type of company
	• principal business activities
	• details of officers
	• details of issued shares and their holders
	• particulars of those who have ceased to be members since the last return.
Accounting records	The company must keep accounting records containing sufficient information to show and explain the company's transactions. In particular the records must show:
	• details of all money received and spent
	• a record of assets and liabilities
	• statement of inventories at end of year.
	Accounting records need to be retained for six years.

Annual accounts	Companies are required to produce annual accounts including:
	• balance sheet and profit and loss account
	• directors' report stating the amount of any dividend and likely future developments.
	The annual financial statements must be approved and signed on behalf of the board of directors and a copy filed at Companies House.

Companies can file their accounts with Companies House using the online service, as well as their corporation tax return using the HMRC online service.

3 Business formation

The formation process of a business entity will depend on what type of entity it is.

3.1 Sole trader

There are no legal formalities. A sole trader can simply start their business.

The sole trader will need to register with HMRC for self-assessment of income tax.

3.2 Partnership

No formalities are required for a general partnership. Two or more people will agree to run a business together.

The partners may have a partnership agreement which sets out matters such as the share of profits. In the absence of a partnership agreement the provisions of the Partnership Act 1890 will apply.

The partners will need to register with HMRC for self-assessment of income tax.

3.3   Company

There is a formal registration process with Companies House with a number of documents that need to be completed and filed:

- memorandum of association
- application for registration
- statement of capital
- statement of consent to act
- statement of compliance

The person who takes the necessary steps to incorporate a company is known as the promoter.

The company will be required to pay a registration fee.

When a company has been formed it is known as 'incorporated'.

The company must also register for corporation tax with HMRC.

The Streamlined Company Registration Service, which was set up as a collaboration between Companies House and HMRC, allows for new businesses to register their company and also register for tax at the same time. The purpose of the service is to make it easier for new businesses to fulfil their legal obligations by registering with Companies House and HMRC in one go and dispense with the requirement to send duplicate information to both.

 Test your understanding 2

There are a number of important legal differences between companies and partnerships.

Which one of the following statements is not true?

A   There are no formalities required to create a partnership

B   A partnership does not need to register with HMRC to pay income tax

C   Partners in a partnership are personally liable for the debts of the business

D   A partnership must have a partnership agreement

3.4   Pre-incorporation contracts

 Definition

A **pre-incorporation contract** is a contract by a person acting on behalf of an unformed company.

The position is that a company, prior to its incorporation (being formed), does not have contractual capacity and therefore the person who is acting on behalf of the company is personally liable. (This is because a company does not legally exist until it is incorporated.)

In summary, with a pre-incorporation contract:

- The company **cannot ratify or approve** the contract.

- The company is not bound by the contract.

- The company cannot enforce the contract against a third party.

 Test your understanding 3

Irene entered into a pre-incorporation contract on behalf of Cosmo Ltd.

Which one of the following option correctly identifies the person who may enforce the contract and against whom it is enforceable?

A   By and against the company only

B   By and against Irene only

C   By the company and against Irene

3.5   Off-the-shelf companies

An 'off-the-shelf' company is one that has already been formed. Buying off the shelf has a number of advantages and disadvantages:

Advantages	Disadvantages
<ul><li>Cheap and simple to buy.</li><li>Can trade immediately.</li><li>No problem of pre-incorporation contracts.</li><li>Can be more appealing to lenders.</li></ul>	<ul><li>Some documents will need to be submitted to Companies House which will need to be tailored to the company.</li><li>May have unsettled liabilities.</li></ul>

3.6   Business name

The name of a company must comply with the following rules:

- It cannot be the same as another in the index of names.
- It cannot use certain words which are illegal or offensive.
- It must have the Secretary of State's consent to use certain words (e.g. England, Chartered, Royal, National, University, Insurance etc.) or any name suggesting a connection with the government or any local authority.

The business name should be displayed on premises in a prominent position where customers and suppliers have access.

It should also be included on the following business documents:

- letters
- written orders for goods and services
- invoices and receipts
- written demands for payment
- business website.

An active company must display its full registered name at:

- the registered office
- all other locations at which it carries on business
- the place where company records are available for inspection.

4 Summary

In this chapter we have seen the different types of business entities and the implications of each. We've covered a sole trader, a partnership and a company.

Each business entity will have different tax and registration requirements. Some small businesses start off as a sole trader and as they get bigger make the decision to incorporate into a company.

Test your understanding answers

Test your understanding 1

B

An employee is not an example of a business organisation.

Test your understanding 2

D

Many partnerships do have a partnership agreement but this is not a requirement. The partnership does not register with HMRC to pay income tax, it is each of the partners.

Test your understanding 3

B

Only the promoter is liable under a pre-incorporation contract.

The finance function

Introduction

This chapter will focus upon the role of the finance function within an organisation. To gain an appreciation and understanding of this, you first need to understand the different functions within a business, and the role each function plays in contributing to business success. Always remember that no two organisations are identical, and that some business functions may be combined in a smaller organisation. The names used to refer to particular business functions and activities may also differ between organisations.

ASSESSMENT CRITERIA
5.1 The different functions of a business
5.2 The role of the finance function
5.3 How the finance team contributes to the success of an organisation

CONTENTS
1 The functions of a business
2 The role of the finance function
3 How the finance team contributes to the success of a business

1 The functions of a business

It is important to appreciate the different functions that a business may have. These functions will vary from business to business dependent upon what the businesses do. A manufacturing business is likely to have a production department, as well as an inventory management function. A service provider is unlikely to have these functions as it does not need to produce goods or manage its inventory to the same extent. Depending upon the size and complexity of a particular business, some functions noted below may have different titles or be combined with other functions.

1.1 Business functions

Here is a summary of the principal functions that a business may have. It is important to consider how these functions interact with the work of AAT learners working in the finance function.

Operations/production

> **Definition**
>
> **Operations** could be regarded as 'what the business does' on a day to day basis to make its sales. For a manufacturer, typical operational activities include the acquisition of raw materials, their conversion into finished products and the supply of that finished product to the customer. Other activities performed by an operations function include the service operations.

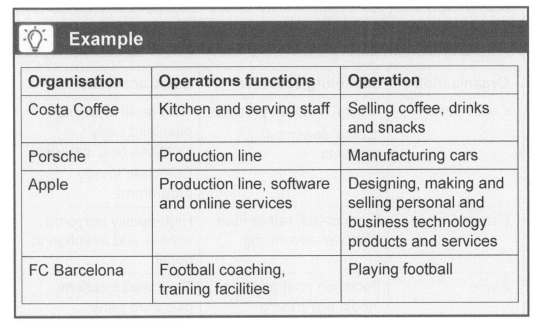

Example

Organisation	Operations functions	Operation
Costa Coffee	Kitchen and serving staff	Selling coffee, drinks and snacks
Porsche	Production line	Manufacturing cars
Apple	Production line, software and online services	Designing, making and selling personal and business technology products and services
FC Barcelona	Football coaching, training facilities	Playing football

The finance function will interact with the production/operations function in a number of ways, such as:

- financing will include costs and monetary values in production budgets

- financing will value inventory counted at the lower of cost and net realisable value

- for a service provider, finance will advise on an appropriate charge-out rate to recover costs incurred.

Marketing and sales

 Definition

Marketing is the promotion and selling of products and services, including market research and advertising activities.

Example

Organisation	Marketing activities	Sales activities
Costa Coffee	'Costa' branded products 'Costa' seasonal products	Own retail locations plus third party locations (e.g. garages) Customer loyalty programme
Porsche	Product-led, rather than 'lifestyle' advertising	High-quality personal service and attention to detail
Apple	Focus on print and media advertising	Own retail locations, plus third party locations (e.g. within department stores) and online
FC Barcelona	Sponsorship and endorsements	Matchday receipts, broadcasting rights, replica kits and souvenirs

The finance function will interact with the marketing and sales function in a number of ways, including:

- financing will prepare budgets for advertising and marketing campaigns, and will monitor and report on the extent of its usage and success

- financing may analyse sales into appropriate classifications, perhaps by geographical area or by product/service type, for the marketing and sales teams to review and identify where sales are increasing or falling.

Human resources management and development

Definition

Human resources management and development comprises all aspects of recruitment, selection, training and development of employees.

Example

Organisation	Human resource management	Human resource development
Costa Coffee	Flexible and part-time working hours available	Training Team ethos
Porsche	Focus on recruiting staff with experience of dealing with high wealth customers	Training and development programme
Apple	Recruitment of 'tech-savvy' and personable individuals	Training Team ethos
FC Barcelona	Extensive scouting and recruitment network for players	Skills and tactics coaching Language training for non-Spanish speaking players

The finance function will interact with the human resources management and development team in a number of ways, such as:

- financing will prepare and process the payroll for all employees

- financing may be asked to prepare a training budget, or to provide costings, when the human resource function has prepared a training requirement plan for the business

- financing may be asked to provide costings for the recruitment of additional employees, or to assess the cost of making some employees redundant.

Information technology

Definition

Information technology comprises the use of computers and telecommunications to store, retrieve and send information.

Example

Organisation	IT hardware	IT software and infrastructure
Costa Coffee	Electronic point-of-sale tills	Linked and secure payment processing Multiple locations linked
Porsche	Employees have IT and support systems to support home working	Software for customers to 'build a car' to individual specifications
Apple	Electronic point-of-sale tills	Linked and secure payment processing, including online Multiple locations linked
FC Barcelona	Multiple terminals and payment points for matchday sales of refreshments and souvenirs	Electronic matchday tickets linked to individuals Online global sales of merchandise

The finance function will interact with the information technology function in a variety of ways, including:

- producing costings and budgets for hardware requirements, whether for additional staff needs, or an upgrade in the hardware specification

- financing may request updated hardware and software to enable staff to do their work more efficiently, or to meet additional information needs

- financing may be asked to oversee and monitor the introduction of new accounts-related software to ensure that it is reliable. This may include the preparation of reconciliations, identification and rectification of errors.

KAPLAN PUBLISHING

Distribution and logistics

 Definition

Distribution is the provision of goods and services to the customer. **Logistics** may be thought of as the overall planning and organisation of distribution, including factors such as storage and inventory control. In effect, distribution and logistics can be considered as doing whatever is required to ensure that the right goods and services are delivered to the right customers in the right location.

Example

Organisation	Distribution	Logistics
Costa Coffee	Delivery of products and ingredients to retail outlets	Ensuring that the correct items are delivered to the correct location within the required timescale
Porsche	Ensuring that finished vehicles are delivered to sales outlets and customers when required	Arrangement of freight and transport of finished vehicles to sales outlets and customers
Apple	Distribution of the appropriate product range and models to the appropriate sales outlet	Ensuring the customers receive the correct item by the agreed delivery date
FC Barcelona	Distribution of merchandise product ranges to sales outlets, whether in the stadium on match days, or to external retail outlets	Ensuring that products are available to purchase and can be paid for at multiple locations during times of peak sales, such as match days

The finance function will interact with the distribution and logistics function in a variety of ways, including:

- recording the delivery of products to sales locations to monitor usage and inventory levels

- making payment to external transporters when deliveries have been made, or when customers have taken delivery at another agreed location.

1.2 Contributing towards business success

All functions must operate efficiently and in harmony with each other if a business is to be successful.

For example, if raw materials and components are not in the right place, production delays may result, which is inconvenient and expensive for a business. Product distribution and logistics may need to be rearranged, and customers may not receive their products by the agreed date.

Similarly, a business needs to recruit, train and retain employees with the appropriate skills and competences across the various business functions to operate efficiently. There is little point in having an exceptional product if the business is unable to distribute it to markets and customers, or there are repeated failures of delivery.

Different business functions working in harmony promotes reliability and certainty and encourages efficiency. All of these factors contribute to achieving, maintaining and improving profitability.

1.3 Interconnected technology to support the business

One common feature of most businesses of all sizes is the increasing use of technology to connect different business activities and functions.

Multi-site retailers use electronic point-of sale systems not only to record sales, but also to record cash receipts or capture debit and credit card details to support payments, to update inventory records and to initiate reordering and delivery of replacement items.

Manufacturing companies may use computer-assisted design technology to develop new products. This is often achieved by teams of individuals working remotely, rather than designers having to be in the same location and proximity. The technology must be reliable and secure to enable access and use only by suitably authorised individuals.

We can now move on to consider the role of the finance function in more detail.

2 The role of the finance function

It is important to understand the range and scope of the finance function of a business. Although the size, structure and number of personnel will differ from one business to another, the finance functions of most businesses are likely to have several common elements and similarities.

2.1 Responsibilities of the finance function

The specific responsibilities of the finance function will differ from business to business. The responsibilities may be split between:

– those which are relevant to external stakeholders, and

– those which are internal to the business.

Responsibilities which are relevant to **external** stakeholders include:

- **producing the statutory financial statements** – a limited company has a legal responsibility to prepare annual financial statements which are issued to its shareholders

- **producing and filing other returns and documents required by law** – all businesses have a responsibility to produce and file information that may be required by law. For example, this could include periodic returns for value added tax if the business is appropriately registered. It could also include regular returns to account for income tax deducted from employees' pay under the PAYE system in the UK.

Responsibilities which are relevant to **internal** stakeholders include:

- **recording transactions** – including purchases, sales, payroll, cash receipts, payments, accruals and prepayments

- **banking of cash and receipts** – this will be mainly sales receipts from customers, but could also include the proceeds of asset disposals, or refunds of tax or value added tax

- **maintaining the accounting records and general ledger accounts** – this could include producing a trial balance before preparing management accounts or the annual financial statements

- **producing information to assist and support other parts of the business** – this could include producing a summary of cheques and remittances received so that the sales department is aware of which credit customers have paid all or part of the amount due

- **producing management accounts and supporting information** – this helps managers to understand how the business is performing and to support decision-making

- **producing summaries and reconciliations** – including bank reconciliations and reconciliations between the receivables' and payables' ledger control accounts with their respective list of individual personal account balances. Where errors are identified, they will then be investigated and corrected.

In addition, the finance function may provide guidance, advice or information to other business functions, or to outside stakeholders. The cashiers' or treasury (as well as the sales) departments may need to know whether any direct remittances were received from customers and, if so, how many and what value from each customer.

Credit customers may contact the finance department to confirm how much is due for payment and whether they could have the bank account details of the business so that they can make direct payment.

A supplier may contact the finance department to query when it can expect to receive payment for an amount outstanding or overdue.

2.2 Interaction with other functions of the business

The finance function may prepare information to support management control and decision-making activities. For example, a budget or financial forecast for the business as a whole could be prepared by the finance team. This will be useful information for the board of directors or senior management who review and evaluate business performance.

In addition to this, the budget or forecast will be broken down into departmental or functional budgets for which the relevant departmental head will take responsibility. A departmental head will not usually need to have a direct interest or knowledge in the budget, target or performance of another department, unless their activities are interlinked in some way.

Many businesses produce management accounts on a regular basis, typically monthly or quarterly. Management accounts help managers throughout the organisation to assess current financial performance and position. The management accounts may be supported by analyses, summaries and commentary on key points identified by the finance function to support and assist those who do not fully understand financial information.

2.3 Tasks and activities that may be outsourced

In the same way that a business may buy a component to include in a production process rather than manufacture the component itself, it is possible for a business to outsource a number of finance function tasks and activities. Outsourcing will occur when particular knowledge or expertise is required which the business does not have in-house. It may also take place as a way of relieving the work pressure of certain individuals so that they can be freed to concentrate on the tasks and activities that are most important to the business.

The tasks and activities that may be outsourced will depend upon the size and nature of the business, along with the skills and competences of the individuals employed in the business. Examples of tasks and activities that may be outsourced include:

- preparation of the monthly or quarterly returns for value added tax, including calculation of the amount due to be paid, or the refund due

- preparation of the monthly or quarterly management accounts and supporting information for the business to understand its current financial performance and position

- preparation of the annual tax return for the business and calculation of the amount due, along with year-end returns and documents relating to payroll

- some businesses may decide to outsource the internal audit function

- ad hoc investigation work, such as investigation of potential fraud or other irregularities

- preparation of the weekly or monthly payroll, creation of individual payslips plus summaries and totals of the payroll cost and the associated liabilities. Liabilities may be due to the HM Inspector of Taxes and to other third parties when deductions (e.g. charitable donations, trade union fees etc.) have been made from employee earnings.

If tasks and activities are outsourced, the business should take particular care to ensure that the scope of those tasks and activities are clearly identified, defined and communicated. The external organisation selected should be carefully chosen to ensure that they are competent, reliable and trustworthy. For example, if payroll tasks are outsourced, confidentiality of employees' personal data needs to be protected therefore choosing a credible payroll agency is essential.

The business should also monitor the performance of the external organisation used to provide outsourced services. This will help to ensure that the external organisation is doing what it agreed to do and, in the event of any problems, the issue can be identified, quantified, discussed and acted upon.

3 How the finance team contributes to the success of the business

3.1   Effective communication

Effective business relationships are based upon honesty, mutual trust and good communication. If the finance team is to make a positive contribution to the success of a business, it cannot work in isolation. It must establish and maintain effective working relationships with other parts of the business and outsiders. This usually involves establishing good inter-personal relationships between individuals working in different parts of the business and external parties.

Good communication is the process of passing information and understanding from one person to another person (or group of people).

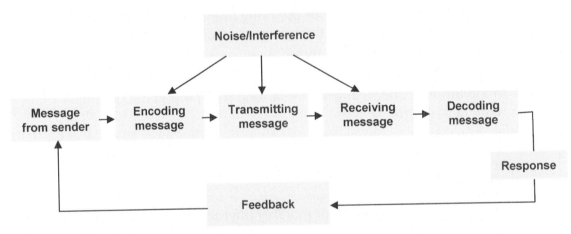

It is important that all elements of the communication process are effective and appropriate or else the communication process may fail.

Encoding a message is the sender deciding what information needs to be communicated.

Transmitting a message is the means of communication used, e.g. verbal, email, or written document.

Decoding a message is the recipient receiving and understanding the message. The language used should be professional and the use of 'jargon' or technical language avoided unless it is appropriate to the recipient.

The response is any reaction or feedback to the message. It may be a simple acknowledgement of receipt and that the message is understood. It could also be a request for clarification or additional information that the recipient requires.

Noise or interference is anything that undermines or prevents the successful transmission of a message. For example, a poorly worded or structured written document may make it difficult to understand, or when background noise or visual distraction in a face-to-face meetings causes problems. Unreliable wifi or insecure electronic communication links may also prevent successful transmission of messages.

Effective communication needs to be clear, complete, accurate, timely and concise. The means of communication should also be appropriate and match the needs of the recipient. For example, if there is an urgent, time-critical requirement for information, sending a hard-copy document in the mail is unlikely to be effective.

Security and confidentiality issues should also be considered when deciding upon the manner of communication. It is important to ensure that an unauthorised person cannot access confidential or sensitive information. As more people adapt to working from home as part of their employment , this issue is of growing importance.

3.2   Finance staff supporting efficient working practices

Efficient working practices require planning and understanding of the information that is required, when it is required, by whom and in what format should it be produced to assist with control and decision-making in the business.

Usually, this involves having routines for tasks and activities to be completed, and ensuring that there is adequate time and resource available to complete the work required. For example, a junior member of the finance function may have the responsibility to perform a bank reconciliation at each month-end, which may take, perhaps, two hours to complete. If it also needs to be reviewed and approved by a manager within a specified period, both the junior member of the team and the manager must plan to allow sufficient time for the work to be done.

The same principle applies to all tasks and activities which the finance function is required to perform. For example, a business may have a schedule of meetings of senior managers to discuss the financial performance of the business based upon the latest set of management accounts. The finance function must therefore plan to collate and produce the information required in advance of those meetings, and to circulate it to the relevant managers. If this is not done, managers will not be in a position to discuss the latest financial results, and nor will they be able to make timely decisions to control and manage the business.

Effective planning and routines help the finance function to have efficient working practices, to monitor and preserve the solvency of the business and to comply with legal and regulatory obligations.

Solvency and long-term financial stability

 Definition

Solvency refers to the financial ability of a business to pay its debts as they fall due (such as paying payables on time). Therefore, the business must ensure that it has cash available to meet these obligations.

Two components of the finance function must therefore cooperate to help ensure the solvency and financial stability of the business.

Management accounting is concerned with the allocation and control of resources.

Financial accounting is concerned with the classification and recording of transactions, maintaining accounting records and ledgers and producing the annual financial statements.

The management accounting team produces cash flow forecasts based upon information from the financial accounting function. The information provided by the finance function for this purpose would include day-to-day operational expenditure and income summaries and plans regarding future investment in non-current assets, dividends and taxation payments, including VAT.

This has an effect on the overall **solvency** of the business.

Ways to ensure and improve financial solvency

- Regular reconciliation of bank balances e.g. to highlight bank charges, interest (both paid and received), direct debits going out and BACS receipts from customers.

- Awareness of the current position of the bank balances e.g. you know if you are likely to go overdrawn and can therefore plan for any charges, or find other ways to avoid an overdraft.

- Regular checks of how much is owed to the business e.g. Sales Ledger Control Account.

- Credit control measures e.g. chasing amounts overdue from customers.

- Monitoring of amounts owing e.g. long-term obligations (loans or mortgages) and when they are due for repayment.

- Review of payments to suppliers e.g. current liabilities and when due.

- Completing weekly payments to suppliers e.g. taking advantage of credit terms and ensuring that the company is making full use of free credit and discounts available.

- Awareness of forward planning e.g. cash flow statements – ask suppliers to extend credit terms and/or renegotiate bank loans and overdraft facilities if you expect to have difficulties paying liabilities in time.

- Consider delaying payments which are not essential, such as the purchase of non-current assets or dividend payments.

It is critical for the ongoing existence of a business that it monitors and manages its activities to remain solvent. Even if a business is profitable, it may still have a shortage of cash to meet its obligations. If a business sells goods on credit, it would soon run out of cash to pay its suppliers and employees if it did not collect the cash from those customers. Having very high profits but low/no cash is described as over-trading.

Legal and regulatory compliance

Efficient working practices help the business to meet its legal and regulatory obligations, which will vary depending upon the size, complexity and the nature of the businesses operations.

Examples of legal and regulatory compliance, which the finance function is likely to have direct involvement in, include:

- Preparation of annual financial statements for shareholders within a specified timescale (if the business is a limited company).

- Submission of regular VAT returns, along with any payment required, within specified timescales (assuming the business is required to account for VAT).

- Submission of an annual tax return, together with any payment required, within specified timescales.

- Submission of regular returns to account for tax and national insurance deductions from employees' pay.

- Businesses in some industries, such as banking and insurance, are subject to additional regulations that require the preparation and submission of additional information to comply with relevant regulations.

The finance function must plan to have sufficient staff and other resources available to meet these obligations, particularly at peak working times. This may include the hire of temporary staff to assist with the significant volume of work required.

If the business does not prepare and submit information to meet its legal and regulatory commitments within the required timescales, it may be subject to fines and other penalties, along with damaging its reputation.

Policies and procedures affecting finance staff

Businesses normally have a range of policies and procedures that affect all staff and others relevant for finance staff only.

 Definition

A policy sets out the parameters or extent of what is or is not permitted e.g. the annual leave policy may specify how many days of paid leave an employee is entitled to, depending upon their grade and years of service.

A procedure sets out the steps required to perform a particular task or activity, or how a policy is applied. For example, if an employee wants to request annual leave, a written request form may need to be authorised by the employee's line manager in advance.

How are policies and procedures communicated to employees? That will depend partly upon the size, structure and nature of the business. Many organisations have a staff handbook (or equivalent), in either hard copy and/or electronic form, which employees can access. Information is also communicated via induction and other training courses, along with 'on-the-job' learning and communication.

Examples of policies and procedures that affect the business as a whole are as follows:

Policy	Procedure
Reimbursement of expenses incurred	Complete an expenses claim form with evidence of the nature of the expense and amount claimed which should be authorised by a manager
All hours worked should be recorded	This should be recorded by using a clock-card, or timesheet or electronic 'swipe card' upon entry and departure from work
Employees must comply with health and safety requirements	Safe systems and procedures to minimise the risk of accident or injury at work

Examples of policies and procedures that are particularly relevant to the finance function include:

Policy	Procedure
All employees' payroll-related data must remain confidential	Employees must obtain prior authorisation from a senior manager before disclosing confidential information
All payments over a specified amount (e.g. £1,000) should be approved in advance by two senior managers	A payment requisition form should be prepared and approved by two senior managers before payment is made
All accounting records must be retained and safeguarded	Accounting records should be filed and organised as specified (e.g. by date or numerical order) and stored in the specified location
Data and records held electronically should be safeguarded and protected from loss or corruption	Only authorised employees can access, update or delete data or records using specified procedures

The role of finance in CSR reporting

Corporate social responsibility (CSR) is becoming increasingly important to many businesses.

 Definition

Corporate social responsibility (CSR) is a business approach that contributes to sustainable development by delivering economic, social and environmental benefits for all stakeholders. Consequently, many businesses now consider how their operations will affect the environment and future generations.

Ways in which this may be demonstrated include:

- introduction of a paper recycling policy within an office building
- adoption of 'paperless' office procedures
- reduction of business-related travel, perhaps by use of 'virtual' meetings, via Zoom or other telecommunication tools
- introduction of schemes to encourage employees to use public transport, cycle or even walk to work – such as a 'bike to work' scheme whereby a bicycle can be hired or purchased from the business at a low rate and space is provided for it to be kept at work during the day
- introduction of energy saving schemes – whereby lights and heating are turned off when not required
- choosing to deal only with suppliers that have similar CSR values.

This list is not exhaustive and you may well be able to think of other methods by which businesses can operate in a more sustainable way.

Sustainability may well have a significant cost at the outset of implementing CSR policies, and, in past generations, it was often considered to represent an additional, and potentially unnecessary, cost burden to a business. This may explain why some businesses chose not to adopt CSR policies.

However, over time, and as the values of society itself have changed, many organisations recognise that they can reap benefits by following a sustainable path. This includes the recognition, by existing and potential customers, of the stance that the businesses are taking in trying to 'do the right thing'. Investing in sustainability processes is now acknowledged by many to be a key driver to increase sales and business activity over time.

For instance, a business may decide to use only recyclable packaging for its products. There will clearly be a cost to the business to source new packaging supplies and, perhaps, pay more for that packaging. However, this should be offset by the positive effect these actions will have on the environment, and the resulting improved image that they can project to customers and potential customers, who may well switch from a competitor.

The finance function may also play a part in collating and reporting data on CSR issues. It may quantify the time and cost savings achieved as a result of introducing CSR initiatives, such as:

- holding virtual meetings, rather than face-to-face meetings

- the adoption of 'paperless' office procedures

- the cost of purchasing of energy-saving equipment, together with the expected savings in energy costs expected to arise over a period of time.

This information may be reported internally to employees and managers, but also reported to external stakeholders and interested parties. For example, the business may have a website in which it includes reporting on CSR issues.

Test your understanding 1

Review each of the practical situations below, and, using the drop down menu below, match each situation with the corporate social responsibility (CSR) objective that relates to it. You may use a CSR objective more than once.

	Practical situation	CSR objective
1	An organisation has a policy of recruiting new employees from within a fifteen-mile radius of its location.	
2	An organisation has a policy of ensuring that all employees attend one personal development training course each year.	
3	An organisation has recently installed solar panels to the factory roof to generate energy that can be used in the production process.	
4	Employees are permitted two days leave of absence each year to volunteer their time for a charitable good cause.	

Drop-down menu choices:

- Ethical employment practices
- Environmentally-friendly policies
- The local community

4 Summary

In this chapter, we considered the different functions of a business, how they are interconnected and how each function contributes to business success.

We then moved on to consider the role of the finance function in more detail, including how the finance function helps the business to meet its legal responsibilities, and provides information to those who need it, whether within the business or to external stakeholders.

Finally, we considered the nature of business relationships and communication. Associated with this is the development of efficient and effective working practices to ensure that duties and responsibilities are complied with and discharged in a timely manner.

The finance function (and those who work within it) can no longer focus only on its own goals and objectives. It must work together with other business functions to ensure the success of the business overall.

Test your understanding answers

Test your understanding 1

	Practical situation	CSR objective
1	An organisation has a policy of recruiting new employees from within a fifteen-mile radius of its location.	The local community
2	An organisation has a policy of ensuring that all employees attend one personal development training course each year.	Ethical employment practices
3	An organisation has recently installed solar panels to the factory roof to generate energy that can be used in the production process.	Environmentally-friendly practices
4	Employees are permitted two days leave of absence each year to volunteer their time for a charitable good cause.	The local community

Business communication and planning

7

Introduction

In this chapter, you will learn to distinguish between different types of information and to choose information for different purposes. You will develop written communication skills and recognise the impact and consequences of ineffective communication. Finally, you will learn how to plan, prioritise, monitor and review your workload.

ASSESSMENT CRITERIA	CONTENTS
6.1 Sources of information	1 Sources of information
6.2 Communicate information	2 Communication of information
6.3 Plan workload to meet the needs of the organisation	3 Planning workloads
	4 Planning methods
	5 Time management
	6 Difficulties in meeting deadlines

1 Sources of information

It is important to develop knowledge and understanding relating to different types and sources of information. Some items of information may be more (or less) reliable or relevant than others, which may affect actions taken and have consequences for the business.

1.1 Valid and invalid information

 Definition

Data is unorganised or unstructured facts or statistics. Data has no meaning unless it is arranged, structured or refined into information. An example of data would be a list of exam marks.

Information is data that is organised or structured, therefore providing context for understanding and decision-making. Using the example of a list of exam marks, that data may be converted into information by matching marks against student names and/or dividing the marks achieved into 'pass' or 'fail' grades.

Valid information is information that is reliable or credible. This could be in terms of accuracy or reasonableness when based upon assumptions or estimates. For example, a set of exam marks matched against student names, with each graded as 'pass' or 'fail' and reviewed to ensure that there are no errors.

Knowledge is the ability to use information to achieve objectives.

1.2 Sources of information

Data may be obtained from either primary or secondary sources. Those sources of data could also be classified as either internal or external sources. When the data has been organised or structured in some way, it then becomes information and is useful.

Primary sources of data are created at the time an event occurs. An example would be notes or minutes taken during a meeting. The notes or minutes could be structured or referenced to make them more informative to users.

Primary data is normally collected for a specific purpose. A business could ask for information and documentation from a new customer who is requesting, say, thirty days credit. The information supplied will help the business decide whether credit should be granted to the new customer and what the credit limit should be.

Secondary sources of data are anything other than primary sources. Normally, it is not collected for a specific purpose and it may be used in a number of different ways or for different purposes. Using the example of a new customer requesting credit, rather than obtaining primary data directly from the new customer, the business could review press reports and official business notices and use those as the basis for its assessment of whether to grant credit and what the credit limit should be.

Internal sources of data and information are obtained, as it suggests, from within the business. Examples of internal sources of data and information include the following:

- personal details of employees maintained by the human resources department such as home address, date of birth, employment start date, job title and grade

- details of suppliers, including location, contact details and a record of purchases made in the current accounting year

- a register of non-current assets which itemises the date of purchase, cost, depreciation method and rate and the location of each asset.

External sources of data and information are obtained, as it suggests, from outside the business. Examples of external sources of data and information include the following:

- published government statistics such as the rate of inflation, the level of unemployment or the national population census

- government legislation, such as employment law, health and safety in the workplace or income and corporation tax law

- newspapers and magazines.

If identical or comparable information is obtained from more than one source, that information becomes corroborated and more reliable. For example, a business will process transactions through its bank account. How do you know that the bank account balance in the general ledger is correctly stated at the end of each month? If the total of debits and credits in the month-end trial balance agree, that provides some assurance that the bank account balance is fairly stated, but it is not foolproof. If a bank reconciliation is performed, information from an external source (the bank statement) is used to help corroborate or verify that the bank account balance in the general ledger is fairly stated.

It is possible that information obtained from more than one source conflicts or cannot be reconciled. Which is the more reliable? In that situation, both sources of information should be investigated to establish which is the more reliable, perhaps because errors have been identified in one source.

The source of information should always be considered when assessing its reliability and credibility. For example, is health advice obtained via a social media site more (or less) reliable than requesting the same advice from a doctor? It is possible that, on occasion, both sources provide the same advice in response to a query. However, there is a greater risk that advice from a social media site is less reliable as you do not know the background, qualifications and experience of whoever provided the advice.

Being aware of the sources of information, together with an assessment of their reliability, will help you to choose the appropriate information for a specific purpose and assist in your decision making. Errors or omissions may be contained within information received which could be the result of unintentional error, or deliberate fraud/manipulation to misrepresent a situation. Information from more than one source that can be verified or reconciled will reduce the risk of error or omission within that information and will help individuals and businesses to make appropriate decisions.

2 Communication of information

Communication of information includes both receiving and transmitting information. Information can be communicated orally, in writing or visually. Often, more than one means of communication is used, such as when attending a product presentation event. There may be a printed product brochure available to read and a practical demonstration of the product to watch along with a narrative explanation from the presenter.

Which form of communication is the most reliable? That will depend upon the circumstances and a range of variables, including:

- the volume of information – if there is more information to communicate, it will probably be better in written, rather than oral form

- the amount of detail or complexity in the information – this information will typically be better communicated in written form as it is permanent and can be accessed more than once

- the period of time over which the information needs to be retained and accessed – the longer the period of time, the more likely that written communication will be most effective.

The nature of the written communication may be formal, such as a report, or less formal, such as a memorandum or a handwritten note for a colleague. Oral communication is typically most appropriate in situations where the information communicated is brief, not very detailed and only required for a short period. As noted in the example of the product presentation above, if more than one communication method is used together, it is more likely to be effective.

2.1 Effective note-taking and documenting information

Even with information communicated orally, it may still be advisable to document it in writing as it provides an immediate and more permanent record of what was communicated, rather than having to rely upon memory later.

Before various forms of communication are considered in turn, it is worthwhile to consider two additional points:

- is there a standard house style or format that should be used to communicate information? If so, that format should be used and it will probably be documented within the organisation handbook or policy documents.

- is the information confidential or commercially sensitive? If so, extra care should be taken to ensure that only the required information is communicated and that it is transmitted to the appropriate person or group.

In many businesses, all of the documents referred to in the following sections would usually be produced using word processing software. Memos and short reports should follow your business's style (house style).

Notes

Probably the most simple and informal method of reporting information to another person is by way of a note.

There is no set format for a note although obviously it must be addressed to the appropriate person, be dated and be headed up correctly so that the recipient knows what it is about. You should also include your name so that the recipient knows who it is from.

In most cases the information that you are reporting on will be important management information and therefore it is unlikely that a note would be the most appropriate format. Only use a note if specifically asked to by the person requesting the information.

Letter

A letter is a more formal method of communication used to communicate with those outside of the business. However, if a business has more than one location, it may still be appropriate to use a letter. Due to the time it takes to communicate via a letter in the postal system, so-called 'snail mail' has been superseded by various forms of electronic mail.

A letter should always have a heading showing the organisation's name, address, telephone number etc. Most organisations will have pre-printed letterheads for you to use (an example of 'House Style').

There are a number of **rules** that should be used when writing a formal or business letter:

- Try to write as simply and clearly as possible and do not make the letter longer than necessary.

- Remember not to use informal language like abbreviations – I'M, CAN'T, HAVEN'T – these should, of course, be written as: I am, cannot, have not...

- Your address – The return address should be written in the top right-hand corner of the letter.

- Date – Different people put the date on different sides of the page. You can write this on the right, parallel with the last line of the address to which you are sending the letter, or on the left 2 lines below the address you are writing to. Write the month as a word (in full).

- Salutation or greeting: Dear Sir or Madam, – If the name of the person to whom the communication is being sent is not known, use this. However, it is always advisable to try to find out a name. When using Dear Sir/Madam the closing will be Yours faithfully.

- Dear Mr Jenkins, – If the name is known, use the title (Mr, Mrs, Miss or Ms, Dr, Prof. etc.) and the surname only. When writing to a woman and it is not known if she uses Mrs or Miss, Ms would be acceptable, (this is used for married and single women). Always use the preferred title of the intended recipient, if the name is known. In this case the closing will be Yours sincerely.

- Signature – the letter should be signed, and the name of the sender printed beneath the signature. If it is unclear if the sender is male or female, then the sender's title should be shown in brackets after the name. If appropriate the job title could also be shown below the name.

KAPLAN PUBLISHING

Electronic mail

The operations and activities of most organisations are computerised and their employees can communicate with each other via email. Email is used to communicate with others, either within or outside of the organisation.

An email must be addressed to the person to whom it is being sent using their email address. It should also be given a title so that the recipient can see at a glance who it is from and what it is about.

In terms of format of the content of the email there are no rules other than any organisational procedures that should be followed.

Take care to ensure that the email is properly addressed to the intended recipient. Most users tend to send many emails to many people and it is easy to pick the wrong recipient from a list. Particular care needs to be taken if your email address book contains several similar names or business addresses, such as individuals with the same surname, or there is another business who has several employees you communicate with regarding different issues.

It is also essential to take care to preserve confidentiality – customer and supplier email addresses should be kept confidential, unless they are already in the public domain. Therefore if you are sending any form of mass email communication, it is important to use the BCC (or blind copy) function. By using this you are ensuring that none of the recipients can see who else the communication has been sent to.

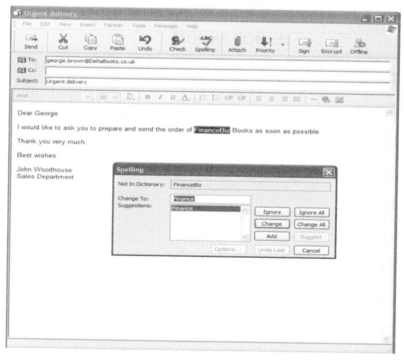

Always spell check your emails before sending them!

Common spelling errors to check for include: to/too; their/there; lose/loose.

Also check your email for sense and tone. It is easy for the tone in an email to be misunderstood by the recipient.

Memorandum

 Definition

A **memorandum** (or memo) is a written communication between two persons within an organisation. The plural of memorandum is memoranda.

A memorandum serves a similar purpose to a letter. However, the main difference is that a letter is usually sent to persons outside the organisation, whereas memoranda or memos are for communication within the organisation itself. Memos can range from brief handwritten notes, to typed sets of instructions to a junior, to a more formal report to a superior. In general, a memo can be used for any purpose where written communication is necessary within the organisation, provided this complies with the policies and procedures of the organisation.

Many organisations will have pre-printed memo forms. In smaller organisations, individual employees may draft their own memoranda. However, there are a number of key elements in any memorandum. All memoranda will show who it is being sent to and who it is from. The date and a suitable reference, for filing purposes, are also essential. The memorandum then must be given a heading to identify its essential content.

MEMORANDUM

Head of
memorandum

To:

From:

Date:

Ref:

Subject:

Body of
memorandum

Signature:

cc:

Enc:

Here is an example of an internal memo.

INTERNAL MEMO

To: B Forster, Accounts Assistant

From: A N Accountant, General Manager

Date: 28 October 20X4

Subject: Budgeted production costs for 20X5

As you know, we have started our budgetary planning exercise for 20X5.

I understand that you have been working on the analysis of budgeted production costs.

Could you please pull together all the information you have gathered and carry out the allocation and apportionment exercise for production overhead costs for 20X5.

We will then have the necessary information that we need to calculate the pre-determined overhead absorption rates for 20X5.

Thanks.

A N Accountant

The content of the body of the memorandum will be discussed in the following paragraph. Whether or not a memo is signed will depend upon the organisation's policy. Some organisations require a signature on a memorandum, whilst others do not.

It is highly likely that a number of copies of the memo will be sent to people in the organisation other than the main person that it is addressed to and these people copied in should be listed in the section marked 'cc'. Finally, if there are any enclosures i.e. additional pieces of information or email attachments sent out with the memorandum, then they should be noted under this final heading of Enc.

The details of the content and style of a memo will depend upon who is sending the memo, to whom they are sending it, the degree of formality required and the subject matter of the memo.

Some memos will simply be handwritten notes from one colleague to another.

If a memo is to be sent to a superior in the organisation, either showing information requested or making recommendations, then both the tone and the content will probably be slightly more formal.

Similarly, if a manager is writing to junior personnel within the department the style adopted may be of a more formal nature, when compared with to another manager within the organisation.

Whatever the precise style and content of the memo, some general rules apply:

- there should be a heading to give an indication of the subject matter

- there should be an introductory paragraph setting the scene

- the main paragraphs of the memo should follow in a logical order, so that the recipient clearly understands the information being communicated, and

- there should be a summary of the main points.

Report

Accountants are used to dealing with figures, but they must also learn to express themselves clearly in words. Accountants are (or should be) well prepared for the degree of precision and organisation required in report writing, but may need practice to improve their written style.

Guidelines for report writing are as follows:

(a) Reporting objectives

Every report has several objectives. Generally, these will be to:

- define the problem

- consider courses of action or alternatives

- make a reasoned recommendation for a specific course of action.

(b) Recipient

The writer should consider the position of the recipient and design the report accordingly. Some recipients will require detailed content; others will have little time to study a lengthy report and should therefore be given one which is as concise as possible whilst still providing all the required information.

(c) Heading

Each report should be headed to show who it is from (or rather, who it has been prepared by) and who it is to, the subject and the date.

(d)   Content

A simple report will begin with a short introduction explaining the reason for its production. There may also be an 'Executive Summary', which, if present, would appear before the introduction. This is a brief summary of the key content of the report which can help readers to decide if it is of use to them (and therefore if they should read the whole report). This will be followed by the body of the report detailing the main issues and discussions. Finally, there will be a conclusion and recommendations made.

(e)   Possible report sections

- Contents
- Executive summary
- Introduction
- Main body with main discussion points
- Conclusions and recommendations
- Appendices (referred to within the report and containing detailed figures and sources of information).

(f)   Paragraph point system – each paragraph should make a point; each point should have a paragraph

This simple rule should always be observed. Important points may be underlined.

(g)   Jargon and technical terms

The use of jargon or technical terms should be avoided, or used only if necessary. If it is necessary to use technical terms, they should be defined, as should any techniques with which the recipient may be unfamiliar e.g. decision trees, linear programming, marginal costing, etc.

This is likely to be the case if an accountant is communicating financial information to others who do not have the same level of knowledge and familiarity with financial terms and concepts.

(h)   Conclusion and recommendations

A report should always reach a conclusion. The conclusion should be stated clearly at the **end of the report**. The report should make clear the basis or justification for arriving at the stated conclusion. It is not enough to simply state all the alternatives and then to recommend a course of action without justification.

(i) Figures

All detailed figures and calculations should be relegated to appendices, with only the main results appearing in the body of the report. Remember that comparative figures will often be useful. The report should be made as visually stimulating as possible, for instance, by the use of graphs or charts instead of, or to supplement, figures.

REPORT

To: Managing Director

From: Candidate

Date: 10 Dec 20X5

Subject: Net Present Value technique

The Net Present Value technique relies on discounting relevant cash flows at an appropriate rate of return. It would be helpful to know:

1   Whether there are any additional cash flows beyond year five.

2   Whether the introduction of a new product will affect sales of the existing products E, C and R.

On the basis of the information provided, the project has a positive Net Present Value of £28,600 and we should therefore proceed.

Spreadsheets

Many businesses use spreadsheets to arrange and classify data for a range of purposes. Like any other business document, it should be properly headed or titled and there may be 'house rules' or a 'house style' for the organisation which should be adopted.

There are a number of principles that can be applied to the creation, update and use of spreadsheets as follows:

- introduction – purpose of the spreadsheet, guide or key to locate items, creator name, date and version number
- separate clearly the inputs, calculations and outputs
- use formulae consistently
- label rows and columns clearly
- ensure that the outputs can be clearly identified

- consider who, and to what extent, others can access and amend the spreadsheet; it may be appropriate to make the document 'read only' or 'comment only' to control any amendments made

- if data is confidential or commercially sensitive, it should be password protected', with the password circulated only to appropriate persons via a separate document or message

- ensure that there is a back-up and version control procedure.

Most spreadsheets will be accompanied by a document that explains the purpose of the spreadsheet, how it was created or designed, references to the key elements of the spreadsheet, outputs and conclusions. This allows recipients to focus only on those parts of the spreadsheet relevant to them. For example, some users may be particularly interested to ensure that the inputs are reliable and that the calculations are accurate. Other users will be primarily interested in the outputs and results, and not too concerned with the underlying inputs and calculations.

Social media communication

This is a form of communication that is easily accessible to many people inside and external to the organisation. It is quite informal and something which an organisation has little control over.

Many organisations try to control or manage communication relating to it on social media. It may permit only nominated individuals to post on social media on behalf of the organisation, or require that an appropriate person approve any social media posting on behalf of the organisation in advance. The tone and manner of communication is professional, with efforts made to ensure that anything posted is factually accurate and reliable.

What an organisation cannot do is control social media postings by anyone external to the organisation. For example, if an individual decides to post false or misleading reviews of products purchased or restaurants visited, it is difficult for an organisation to counter this. Whilst they may post a response to the review, it may not be regarded as a satisfactory resolution of the issue.

Social media can be a useful business tool. Many businesses undertake publicity, marketing and selling activities using social media sites. New businesses in particular may find that social media is a cost-effective method of making consumers aware of their products and services. However, always remember that the principles of good communication practice should be applied.

An organisation may also have staff policies that forbid or control the posting of work-related content on social media sites. Breach of these policies may leave an employee liable to disciplinary action. Any postings that are inaccurate or inappropriate may leave the organisation open to legal action and consequent penalties. At the very least, there is likely to be adverse publicity for the organisation.

Intranet

 Definition

An intranet is a computer network for sharing information, collaboration tools, operational systems, and other computing services within an organisation, usually excluding access by outsiders.

Many businesses have an intranet. Usually, access to it requires employees to log on to the system using their individual credentials. It will then give access to a range of data and information, such as:

- business organisation policies and procedures

- standard forms and documentation, such as expense claim forms

- business updates and newsletters for employees

- employee directory – contact details, such as name, location, department, job title.

Some parts of the intranet may have restricted access. For example certain financial or payroll information may only be accessible by senior managers using their personal login credentials.

Communication tends to be primarily from the business to the employees, with links for the employee to access relevant information, or even to communicate with identified or nominated individuals. Consequently, the tone and form of communication tends to be formal, but could also be informal where, for example, the intranet may include a section for staff to post personal photos or stories they would like to share with colleagues.

2.2 The consequences of inappropriate information sharing

Care should be taken to avoid the risk of inappropriate information sharing. In its mildest form it may have no immediate or long-term consequences, other than, perhaps, personal embarrassment for the sender. For example, if a product price list is sent to the wrong customer it may not be a significant issue as the price list is normally freely available information that the organisation is happy to make available to anyone.

However, the circulation or communication of information that is commercially sensitive or confidential may have more serious consequences. Accountants are used to dealing with commercially sensitive or confidential information, so it is important that this degree of familiarity does not lead to complacency and inappropriate communication of information.

Most countries, including the UK, are subject to a range of laws and regulations relating to how data is acquired, stored, accessed and used. The key principle of this law and regulation is to ensure the confidentiality and appropriate use of data that is personal and identifiable and which could be misused if accessed.

The General Data Protection Regulation (GDPR) in the UK enables a range of sanctions to be imposed by the Information Commissioner for breach of regulations, including:

- warnings and reprimands
- a temporary or permanent ban on data processing
- ordering amendment, restriction or deletion of data
- suspending data transfers to third parties
- significant fines.

Additionally, an organisation may be liable to legal action by aggrieved parties who consider that there has been inappropriate disclosure of information.

It is also important to remember that inappropriate disclosure of information may occur within an organisation. If payroll data was disclosed to others in the organisation who do not have a genuine business need to see it, this would be very embarrassing for the affected individuals, the person who was responsible for the inappropriate disclosure and the organisation as a whole.

The individual responsible for inappropriate communication of confidential or commercially sensitive information may be subject to a range of consequences including:

- warning or reprimand
- adverse review and appraisal outcomes
- suspension
- dismissal.

3 Planning workloads

The planning of workloads is important if individuals, teams, departments and the organisation as a whole are to meet deadlines and operate efficiently. The ability to do this requires an understanding of not only an individual's own deadlines, but the deadlines of others who are dependent on that individual to provide information.

3.1 Planning and organising

All levels of management are involved in planning. At the highest level, decisions are made on strategy. Further down the organisational hierarchy, the plan is fleshed out to determine how and when the strategic objectives are achieved.

Organising is the next stage after planning. It means working out the specific jobs or tasks that must be completed in order to fulfil the plans agreed upon, grouping activities into a pattern or structure, giving specific jobs to people in the organisation and setting deadlines for their completion.

At the individual level, work planning involves scheduling and timetabling ongoing routine tasks so that they will be completed at the usual time, whilst also completing the high priority tasks arising from any new specific job or task.

The basic steps and objectives in work planning include the following:

The establishment and effective treatment of priorities (considering tasks in order of importance for the objective concerned).

Scheduling or timetabling tasks and allocating them to different individuals within appropriate timescales, (e.g. continuous routine work and arrangements for priority work with short-term deadlines), to achieve work deadlines and attain goals.

Coordinating individual tasks within the duties of single employees or within the activities of groups of individuals.

Establishing checks and controls to ensure that priority deadlines are being met and work is not 'falling behind', and that routine tasks are achieving their objectives.

Agreeing the mechanism and means to reschedule ordinary work to facilitate and accommodate new, additional or emergency work by drawing up 'contingency plans' for unscheduled events. Because nothing goes exactly according to plan, one feature of good planning is to make arrangements for what should be done if there were a major upset, e.g. if the company's computer were to break down, or if the major supplier of key raw materials were to go bust. The major problems for which contingency plans might be made are events that, although unlikely, stand a slim chance of actually happening.

The tasks you complete at work will fall into four categories:

1   **Daily**, e.g. routine tasks such as recording sales invoices in the sales day book or recording cash received.

2   **Weekly**, e.g. preparing journal entries to post totals from books of prime entry to the nominal ledger.

3   **Monthly**, e.g. bank reconciliation or sales ledger reconciliation.

4   **One-off**, e.g. information for a report.

Most employees in an organisation will spend the majority of their time working on the routine tasks that are part of their role and responsibilities. However, at times, unexpected and non-routine tasks may arise. These tasks need to be accommodated without them affecting routine responsibilities or compromising deadlines.

The performance criterion states that you should:

- plan and prioritise tasks according to organisational procedures and regulatory requirements

- prioritise and make changes to priorities, resources allocations and work plans accordingly

- review workloads to identify potential bottlenecks and problems so that you can alert colleagues and obtain the necessary support

- check that work methods and activities conform to legal and regulatory requirements and organisational procedures.

3.2 Agreeing timescales

The planning of work requires the allocation of time to the components of the work to be completed. This must be performed for the organisation as a whole, to individual departments and sections, and to individual employees. Planning must be based on periods of time, and the degree of flexibility built into planning will vary according to the length of time being planned for. The principles of planning will require:

(a) determining the length of time covered by the plans

(b) planning by departments and groups of individuals

(c) planning by individuals.

There are three time scales, which are normally involved in planning work:

(a) long-term

(b) medium-term

(c) short-term.

These three terms are really only expressions of convenience. Time is relative. For example, a period of five years might be considered long-term within an organisation producing footwear but short-term in the aviation industry. Three years may be short-term to an organisation as a whole but to a department within that organisation it may be medium-term whilst to an individual employee it may be long-term. It is important that whatever the relevant time period may be to a group or individual, work is allocated accordingly.

3.3 Identifying priorities

Much office work is of a routine nature although there are exceptions. Priorities must be established with regard to the cyclical nature of routine work and unexpected demands.

The cyclical nature of routine work often means that certain tasks have to be completed by a certain time. In such cases other work may have to be left in order to ensure that the task with the approaching deadline date is given priority. Such tasks might include:

- the preparation of payroll sheets for a weekly computer run

- the despatch of monthly statements to account customers

- the checking of stock levels at predetermined intervals and the appropriate action, such as re-ordering.

Unexpected demands are often made at departmental, sectional or individual level. If management requires urgent or additional work to be carried out then, obviously, some other tasks will have to be postponed.

Given that routine tasks may be anticipated and that unexpected demands cannot, this area of priority identification can be divided into routine tasks, which can be accommodated within normal sensible planning, and 'emergency-type' tasks that must be performed at short notice.

Routine work usually includes a number of tasks that, as a matter of course, fall into a natural order in which they should be performed. This 'natural order of events' approach can usually be incorporated into the normal routine of the office and/or the individual to such an extent that often it is not apparent that there has ever been a problem with the identification of priority tasks.

Where tasks/events of an 'emergency' nature arise the main problem facing an individual will be that of deciding which of the routine tasks should be postponed. However, the postponement of one routine task will automatically delay successive tasks.

3.4 Guidelines for determining priorities

In determining priorities, the following should be noted:

- Wherever it is possible for a priority to be anticipated, such as in the case of the 'natural order of events' described above, then associated difficulties will usually be overcome by sensible, logical planning.

- If an 'emergency type' task occurs, then normal routine work will automatically take second place. It is here that decisions must be taken to decide which routine tasks should be postponed. Also, plans should be formulated and implemented to ensure that the routine work being postponed is carried out as soon as possible, resulting in minimum disruption to the normal routine.

Often these situations arise where one priority comes into conflict with another. Here the task deemed more important by a responsible individual should take preference.

Unfortunately, individuals within one department or section are often blinded to the needs of other departments or sections. A task that is classed as low priority within one department or section may be of the utmost priority to another. Thus, in arriving at any decision, the individual making that decision must ensure that the effect on each department is considered when making a decision.

A responsible individual should determine priorities. Often, especially in the matter of routine cycles, the individual responsible for that work will be qualified to determine any priority. However, the greater the effect and the wider the span of influence of priority determination, the more responsible the individual should be.

When an unexpected task is given to you, you must have the flexibility to be able to reschedule your routine work in order to complete this task.

3.5   Setting priorities

Activities need to be sequenced and scheduled. There may be conflict between two planning tasks since the best sequence of activities to put the plan into place might not be consistent with the schedule of when particular activities need to be completed. The sequence of activities may be determined by the following:

- An activity must precede another when it is a pre-requisite for later activities. For example, the assembly of a car cannot precede the manufacture or purchase of its components.

- The sequence of activities may be dictated by the ease with which they can be completed.

- An activity may be considered more important than others. For example, in the building industry priority will be given to outdoor work when the weather is favourable to minimise the risk of delays later.

The organisation's operations require proper scheduling of resources to run efficiently and avoid periods of over or under-utilisation. Some activities must occur at precisely the right time, e.g. a specific day and time slot for advertising a new product. The scheduling of tasks can also affect customer service in terms of delivery.

3.6   Prioritisation of routine tasks

Routine tasks may be tasks that are performed several times each day, once or twice each day, or on a weekly or monthly basis.

Examples of routine tasks might include the following:

- sending out invoices to customers each day

- opening the post at the beginning of the day and again after the second post has arrived

- filing all copy invoices at the end of the week

- preparing a list of outstanding customer balances at the end of each month.

Priorities are tasks listed in order of importance. Each day, employees will need to prioritise the tasks that they are required to complete during that day.

The first job of the day might be to open the post, as the post may contain urgent items to be dealt with by you or other members of the department, or items that are needed in order to perform a later task. This will therefore be a high priority job and should not be left until the middle of the morning.

If your job includes responsibility for sending out invoices to customers then it will be a high priority that these invoices are sent out on the same day as the sale or customer order. The task of filing copies of the invoices is less urgent. It may be possible to leave this until later in the day, or even later in the week.

Another skill you can use to analyse jobs is sequencing. When you put things in sequence, you arrange steps in the order that you perform them. When you work out the sequence to carry out the tasks, you are judging two things:

- How urgent is the task?

- How important is the task?

These are not the same thing. Urgent tasks need to be completed within a particular time frame. Important jobs may affect a lot of people or cost a lot of money. They may also have significant consequences if they are not done, or are done badly.

For example, if you are going abroad on holiday, it is **important** that you have a passport. If your holiday isn't for six months, it isn't **urgent**. It becomes urgent if you leave it too late.

3.7 Prioritisation of unexpected tasks

Unexpected or non-routine tasks will normally occur for one of two reasons:

1 The unexpected tasks may be due to additional activity in the organisation, such as a new product launch or takeover of another company.

2 Unexpected tasks can also occur due to some 'emergency' within the organisation such as a colleague being off work ill, or an error being found which must be dealt with immediately.

They should be fairly easy to identify, as they will normally involve instruction from a more senior member of staff. For example, if a member of your department is off ill, and is unlikely to return for the rest of the week, it is likely that the manager or supervisor will reschedule that person's tasks to be dealt with by the other members of the department.

However, some unexpected tasks might not be so clearly signalled. For example, suppose that you answer the telephone for a colleague during his/her/their lunch break. If the call is from a customer with an urgent request for information, then this customer query may be an unexpected task that you will need to deal with.

If an unexpected task is identified then this must also be prioritised and fitted in with the routine tasks of the individual. Unexpected tasks will not necessarily always be urgent, although many will be. When an unexpected task is identified the individual should ensure that he or she fully understands the following points:

• the precise nature of the task

• the resources or information required to carry out the task

• the time required to obtain those resources or that information

• the time that the task is expected to take (remember that as an unexpected task it is unlikely that the individual will have performed this task before)

• the time allowed for this task and the deadline

• the importance of the task

• the priority it should be allocated in respect of the work being carried out.

Only once aware of all of these points is it possible to correctly prioritise the task and schedule it, together with the remaining routine tasks.

For example, suppose that you are required to produce a report for a Board meeting on Wednesday 12 March. Today is Monday 3 March. In order to produce the report you will require a number of files from the central filing system which are likely to take two days to be accessed and delivered. The manager of the department who has commissioned this report estimates that there will be approximately one full day's work obtaining the relevant information from the files and another half-day in actually preparing the report itself. Owing to backlogs in the typing department your manager suggests that the report is with the typist by next Monday morning, 10 March, at the latest in order that it can be typed, proof read and any adjustments made in time for the Board meeting on Wednesday 12 March.

In this instance, the only task that you will need to perform immediately, a high priority today, is to inform central filing of the files that are required for the report. As the files will not reach you until Wednesday then there can be nothing else done for this task until that day. You must then ensure that during Wednesday, Thursday and Friday approximately a day and a half is set aside to prepare and write the report. You must also ensure that when the report is returned from typing at the beginning of the following week the proof-reading is given a high priority.

As a further example, suppose that a colleague in your department has called in ill this Monday morning. Your manager thinks that your colleague will not return to work this week, and therefore all of his/her/their responsibilities must be dealt with by the other members of the department for the entire week. One of your colleague's responsibilities, which your manager has allocated to you, is to deal with customer complaints. It is the organisation's procedure to ensure that all complaints are dealt with, even if this is simply an acknowledging letter, on the same day as the complaint is received. Therefore, in order to comply with organisational procedures, you will need to give priority to any complaints received in the post each morning and any telephone complaints received during the day. Again, you must ensure that your own priority routine tasks, such as sending out invoices on the day of the order, are completed at the appropriate time.

 Test your understanding 1

List all of your routine daily tasks.

Make a separate list of all non-routine tasks that may arise, and state why they arise. (By their nature non-routine tasks are unexpected and you may need to invent possible non-routine tasks or recall non-routine tasks you were asked to complete on an earlier occasion!)

Tasks not completed within the necessary or expected timescales, may result in consequences (with varying degrees of significance or severity) for the business, including:

- delay in communicating with customers and/or suppliers, resulting in an adverse outcome such as loss or disruption of sales or supplies

- delays for work colleagues who are expecting the output of your completed tasks to be available to them, so that they can progress with their own work. For example, you produce a list of receivables ledger balances by a due date so that a colleague can prepare the month-end reconciliation with the control account balance in the general ledger

- delays for managers and senior members of staff who have responsibility for submitting information and returns to official bodies and regulators within defined timescales e.g. completion of the monthly or quarterly VAT return plus payment, or the monthly return for the deduction of income tax and national insurance from wages and salaries

- you, and/or colleagues, may be required to work additional hours at short notice to complete tasks which may be inconvenient for individuals depending upon their personal circumstances

- you, and/or colleagues, may be required to reorganise work planned in order to accommodate delays encountered elsewhere.

4 Planning methods

4.1 Introduction

Different organisations, groups and individuals have individual characteristics, tastes, styles, preferences and objectives. These particular objectives may well be achieved via different methods and systems of scheduling work.

As a method of planning group work, it is vital that these efforts are coordinated – not only with each other but with all actions required to complete the task. This coordination ensures appropriate communication and support within the group, ensuring that all members of the group progress towards their goal.

The following planning methods and systems are the most common:

(a)   checklists

(b)   bar charts

(c)   bring-forward, bring-up and follow-up systems

(d)   activity scheduling and time scheduling

(e)   action sheets

(f)   other systems, including planning charts and boards, and diaries.

Each of these methods and systems will be discussed individually below.

However, any combination of the above may be in use at any one time within an organisation or by an individual employee.

4.2   Checklists

Checklists are often used and are perhaps the simplest method, being essentially a list of items or activities. The preparation of a typical checklist would involve the following:

(a)   the formulation of a list of activities and tasks to be performed within a given period

(b)   the identification of urgent or priority tasks

(c)   the maintenance of a continuous checklist with the addition of extra activities and tasks as and when required.

This method is obviously limited in its application because of its simplicity. It is suited to mundane or routine tasks that are essential in completing the objective.

Typical uses of checklists include the following:

(a)   purchasing requirements

(b)   points to cover at an interview

(c)   points to cover at a meeting (e.g. an agenda)

(d)   organising a conference or meeting.

Below is an example checklist showing when certain returns associated with PAYE are due.

STATUTORY RETURNS SCHEDULE

Returns	Description	Date Due	Forward To
P60	This is a total of the employee's year-end earnings including Tax and NI.	05.2022	Employee
P9D	Must be completed for all employees earning less than £8,500 (including reimbursed expenses and the taxable values of benefits) and for Directors for whom forms P11D are not required.	07. 2022	Employee and HMRC
P14	Summary of deductions such as Tax, NI, SSP, SMP.	05. 2022	HMRC
P35	Statement of Tax, NI, SSP and SMP for each employee together with an overall summary of the NI monthly or quarterly payments made by the employer in respect of that tax year.	05. 2022	HMRC
P38S	Relates to students who work for an employer during their holidays.	05. 2022	HMRC
WTC	Year-end summary of Working Tax Credits paid to employees throughout the year.	05. 2022	HMRC
DPTC	Year-end summary of Disabled Person's Tax Credit paid to employees throughout the year.	05. 2022	HMRC

4.3 Bar charts

A bar chart has two main purposes:

(a) to display the time necessary for an individual activity

(b) to show visually represent the time differences between different activities.

Bar charts are particularly useful for checking the time schedules for a number of activities that are interdependent. A bar chart for the building of a house extension might be shown over a period of six months and an example is given over the page.

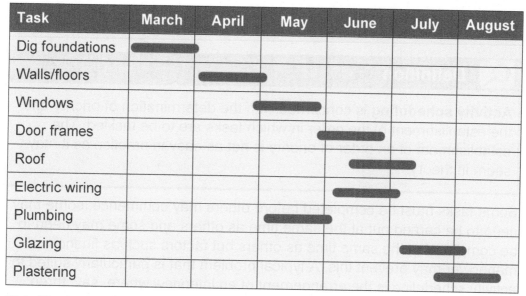

Task	March	April	May	June	July	August
Dig foundations	▬▬▬					
Walls/floors		▬▬▬				
Windows			▬▬▬			
Door frames				▬▬		
Roof				▬▬▬		
Electric wiring				▬▬▬		
Plumbing			▬▬▬			
Glazing					▬▬▬	
Plastering						▬▬▬

This illustrates the importance of bar charts in showing:

(a) overall progress to date, thus assisting in monitoring

(b) the progress attained at an individual stage of a multi-stage process.

4.4 Bring-forward, bring-up and follow-up systems

These systems are more sophisticated than checklists and bar charts. They are particularly useful for coping with documentation. The systems involve recording the detail of the work to be performed and the dates on which this work is to be completed. A routine is established with a view to allocating necessary tasks to the precise day.

The systems all operate around the following principles:

> A note is made of anything to be done in the future, showing details of the appropriate action or format (e.g. make a telephone call or write a letter).

↓

> The note is filed away in a concertina folder with separate files for each day.

↓

> Each appropriate file is checked at the start of each day and the action required that day noted.

↓

> The action is carried out.

4.5 Activity scheduling

 Definition

Activity scheduling is concerned with the determination of priority and the establishment of the order in which tasks are to be tackled. The establishment of an order of priority is not as easy in practice as it may seem in theory.

Some tasks must be completed before others may commence, some may need to be carried out at the same time as others and some may need to be completed at the same time as others but factors such as finance or manpower may prevent this. A typical problem that is particularly suited to activity scheduling is the arrangement of an interview where, say, three panel members are required and six candidates have been short-listed for interview. Obviously, mutually convenient dates must be found when all nine parties are available and the room, which is to be used for the interview, must be free for use on these days.

Activity scheduling involves the identification of key factors and their assembly on a checklist. In the example given above, the two key factors are room availability and people availability. It may be used for any task, which involves a number of actions that must necessarily be undertaken in sequence.

4.6 Time scheduling

 Definition

Time scheduling is an extension of activity scheduling by indicating the required time for each task. It follows the preparation of an activity schedule and involves the determination of time required for each activity.

Given that within an activity schedule some tasks will be performed simultaneously, it should be noted that the total time period over which the series of activities is completed may not equate to the total of the individual activity times.

Effectively, a time schedule determines the order in which activities are scheduled on a checklist, the time required for each activity also being shown alongside each item. Tasks that can be performed in parallel are noted. The total of the individual activity times, with allowances for simultaneous activities, will produce the time allowed for one complete group of activities. Time scheduling is thus particularly useful in the process of planning, especially as it enables the initial deadlines to be set.

4.7 Action sheets

This system is a natural progression from activity and time scheduling. Action sheets summarise the time that the stages of the individual task should take, and contain estimates of the start and finish dates of each stage.

The example below depicts an action sheet for a wedding.

Activity number	Detail	Number of weeks in advance	Certification of completion (initials or signature)
1	Book church	26	
2	Book reception hall	26	
3	Send out invitations	12	
4	Receive replies	4	
5	Order food/refreshments	3	
6	Check arrangements	2	
7	The wedding day	–	

Action sheets are widely used and are often utilised in conjunction with bar charts.

4.8 Planning charts and boards

These usually show information in summary form so that the information may be seen at a glance. They are often used to show details of future events that affect departments (e.g. to plan staff holidays).

4.9 Diaries

Diaries are an obvious and consequently often overlooked aid to planning. They can range from simple handwritten diaries showing an individual's appointments, meetings etc. through to sophisticated computerised diaries, either as part of the organisation's computer network or alternatively in some form of electronic personal organiser. Diaries can also usefully be used, not just to show appointments etc., but also to highlight matters that should be followed up or chased up on a particular date. For example, suppose that you have been involved in a number of telephone discussions with a potential customer. The potential customer has indicated that he/she/they will have decided whether or not to go ahead with an order by Thursday of this week at the latest. You may wish to make a note in your diary for Wednesday to give the potential customer a telephone call in order to determine whether there is any additional information that you can provide them.

Diaries are especially suited to individual employees but only if the employee ensures that all relevant details of any appointments are entered as a matter of course. Recording full details is important because failure to note down complete information regarding a particular appointment could have serious repercussions for the organisation, particularly if an appointment has to be rescheduled or handled by someone else. It is sensible to have a routine for making appointments and indeed to create a 'checklist for appointments'.

 Test your understanding 2

Kim has recently joined a busy administration department in a manufacturing organisation. Kim is slightly shocked that the organisation seems to lack formal procedures and feels that the new job is one of 'fire-fighting'. Once one crisis is over another one arrives. Kim feels there is never a spare moment in the working day between arrival at 9.00am and departure at 5.30pm. Kim is constantly responding to so called 'urgent' requests from other people to: "just do this for me Kim please, it won't take a moment", or "this job's top priority – can you rush it through please?" Every job seems to be "top priority"!

How will this 'Crisis Management' method of working impact on Kim? What are the consequences for Kim's work? What time management techniques could Kim use to help organise and prioritise the workload?

---

5 Time management

5.1 Timetabling tasks

Work planning ensures that commitments to others are met within agreed timescales and necessitates planning and organising on the part of the organisation and the employee.

Your time needs to be properly managed if you are to work efficiently and effectively. The first way to start to organise your time is to plan your use of time.

Example 1

Here is Joe's diary for the coming week:

May 2022				
Monday	Tuesday	Wednesday	Thursday	Friday
1 **9am** Meeting Mr Green	2 **3pm** Group Meeting	3 **2.30pm** Visit other site	4 **Mum's Birthday!**	5

This shows his meetings with other people but not how he will use the rest of his time.

Solution

Here is a more useful version of his diary for the same week:

May 2022

	Monday	Tuesday	Wednesday	Thursday	Friday
9am	**Meeting Mr Green**	Record Cash	Record Cash	Record Cash	Record Cash
10am	Record Cash	Update cash book	Bank reconciliation	Finish bank reconciliation	Prepare cash flash figure
11am					
12pm					
1pm	Lunch	Lunch	Lunch	**Buy card for mum**	Lunch
2pm	Record cash continued	Prepare for meeting	**2.30pm Site Visit**	Prepare info for report	Prepare journals
3pm	Speak to Pat about new system?	**Group meeting**			Count petty cash
4pm	Home early				Request cash

Notice how all the major tasks have been timetabled. Joe has estimated the amount of time to complete each task and blocked out that time. This ensures that Joe has sufficient time to complete tasks before the necessary **deadline**.

5.2 Timing of tasks

Whatever function you perform at work, you will always have tasks to complete, which fall into four categories:

	Category	Examples
1	Daily	Recording cash received.
		Recording sales invoices in sales day book.
		Recording purchase invoices in purchase day book.
2	Weekly	Preparing journal entries to post totals from books of prime entry to nominal ledger.
3	Monthly	Receivables ledger reconciliation.
		Payables ledger reconciliation.
		Bank reconciliation.
4	One-off	Information for reports.

Following from example 1, Joe also keeps a list of quick tasks to complete at appropriate times. As he completes them, he crosses them off his list.

5.3 Review of work plans

Following from example 1, each evening before he goes home, Joe reviews his work schedule and updates it for:

(a)   tasks to carry over

(b)   any other changes (e.g. meeting times changed).

Even if you do not have the opportunity to schedule your work, try scheduling your studies and your free time! You should find that you get more out of your time.

6 Difficulties in meeting deadlines

6.1 Introduction

The syllabus area here is that you 'report anticipated difficulties in meeting deadlines to the appropriate person'. There will always be occasions when, for one reason or another, the deadline or target cannot be met. Often, individuals are vague regarding the information they require, which may mean that wrong or incomplete information is provided. It may be that the deadline cannot be met because of problems encountered by the supplier of the information.

Perhaps, if a student is required to provide some information, they might be unable to gather the information by the deadline because of a lack of sufficient working hours, or due to personal circumstances, such as a medical appointment.

Alternatively, the problems with meeting the deadline may be due to a third party. Perhaps the information required has to be acquired from a third party. If this party fails to provide the information by the deadline you have set, then you are obviously unable to pass this information on by your own deadline.

Identified below are typical examples of problems that may be encountered:

(a)   Files, books, etc. may be borrowed and not returned.

(b)   Reference journals may not be kept up-to-date.

(c)   Access to information may be denied due to security/confidentiality considerations.

(d)   Computer systems may 'crash'.

(e)   International time differences may mean that offices are not open when required.

(f)   Files, books or journals may be incorrectly filed.

(g)   Wrong or insufficient information is provided.

(h)   Delays may occur because information has been archived.

(i)   Unexpected tasks become necessary and take priority.

Whatever the reason for not achieving the target or deadline, it is vital that students understand the importance of reporting and explaining this fact.

6.2   Difficulties are promptly reported

It is tempting, in any situation, to put off dealing with any problems. In a business context, if it appears likely that a deadline will not be met then we may to put off telling the appropriate person about it in the hope that the information can eventually be reported by the required deadline.

This really is the wrong attitude. As far as your manager or colleague, who has requested the information, is concerned, it is far better that he, she or they know of any possible delays at the earliest opportunity. Therefore, we should report the possibility of a missed deadline at an early stage, rather than leaving such news until the last minute. This gives the manager a chance to revise his, her or their plans accordingly.

The rule is that if you become aware of the possibility of missing a deadline for the supply of information, this should be reported immediately. If the circumstances are subsequently change and the information is reported by the deadline this will be a bonus. However, if the anticipated circumstances occur and the information is not available then at least the manager concerned has had advance notification, giving them the chance to plan to work around the problem.

6.3   Explanation of delays

If you are unable to perform a duty by a specified deadline then, not only must this fact be reported, but it must be reported in an appropriate manner – we must consider politeness and professional behaviour.

Even if you believe that the deadline that has been set is impossible to meet, there is nothing to be gained from an aggressive or impolite attitude towards the person requiring the information. There will be instances when deadlines are set that are earlier than is absolutely required, and provided that you give an explanation of the constraints on your time in a reasonable manner, it is possible that the deadline may be extended.

In other circumstances the deadline will be fixed and cannot be extended. Again, any aggressive response will only heighten the displeasure of the manager. The best way to deal with any situation where a deadline is not achieved is to explain politely and rationally why this has happened. This may be, as mentioned earlier, due to personal circumstances or due to delays from third parties.

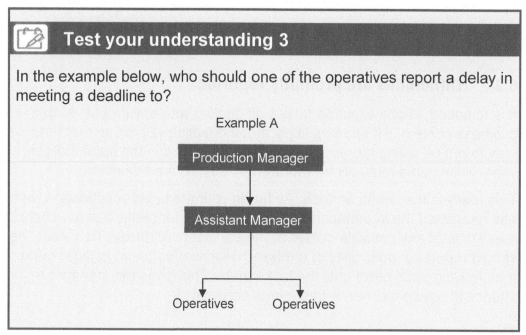

Test your understanding 3

In the example below, who should one of the operatives report a delay in meeting a deadline to?

Example A

Production Manager

Assistant Manager

Operatives   Operatives

Test your understanding 4

Prepare a checklist of information you would collect and retain relating to a meeting at another organisation's premises.

Test your understanding 5

Today is Friday.

Terri has three tasks to complete, each of which will take two hours. Terri's supervisor expects that all tasks will be completed by 10.00am on Monday.

Terri was unable to perform any of the tasks on Friday morning because the computer was not working. It is now 2.00pm on Friday. Terri's working day normally finishes at 5.00pm.

What should Terri do in these circumstances?

A   Complete one of the tasks and start one of the others. Terri should be able to complete all of them by noon on Monday.

B   Complete the most urgent task and take home the other two tasks. Terri is bound to be able to find time to finish them over the weekend.

C   Contact the supervisor immediately and explain the problem. Terri should suggest that the most urgent task should be completed first before starting one of the others.

D   Start all of the tasks and do parts of each of them. This way Terri has at least done something towards each of them before the end of the working day.

7 Summary

This chapter should help you to focus on the way that you manage your own workload. How you plan, prioritise and organise both routine and non-routine work is of critical importance to how efficient and effective you will be.

Now that you have read the chapter you should be aware of the importance of anticipating problems before they arise and asking for assistance where necessary. Identifying any weaknesses in your own skills, level of experience, or ability to meet deadlines is critical to working effectively as a member of a team. The consequences of late or non-delivery of work was also considered within the chapter.

Effective communication requires the use of appropriate oral and written skills, as well as practical issues such as word processing and spreadsheet competencies. A related issue was the importance of ensuring that confidential or commercially sensitive information is communicated only to those who have a genuine reason to receive it and, if in any doubt, prior approval should be obtained from a manager.

Test your understanding answers

 Test your understanding 1

Possible routine tasks for someone working in, for example, payables ledger, could include:

- opening and distributing the post
- taking telephone calls from suppliers
- processing supplier invoices
- posting supplier invoices to payables ledger
- filing all invoices received
- maintaining up-to-date records of the outstanding payables position and when payments are due.

Possible non-routine tasks could include:

- providing up-to-date aged payables analysis to new investor
- raising sales invoices when a colleague is off sick.

 Test your understanding 2

Kim appears to have to always respond to others' demands upon available time and has little control over planning own time or work. The likely impact of this method of working on Kim is that it will be stressful and unsatisfying. The consequences for Kim's work are that it is likely to deteriorate in quality and important deadlines may be missed as others encroach upon the available time.

Kim should learn strict time management techniques such as daily lists and action plans. Kim needs to prioritise tasks perhaps in negotiation with those supplying the task or work requirements. To do this Kim needs to communicate very firmly and clearly with those requesting the task and work to be completed. On the next occasion Kim is asked to do something which is apparently 'top priority', Kim must establish exactly when the work is required by and firmly negotiate a reasonable deadline. Colleagues may then learn to respect that Kim is a busy person who has other demands upon the available time.

Test your understanding 3

The organisation chart shows the assistant manager as the line manager for the operatives. Therefore, if an operative if facing difficulties in meeting a deadline they should raise this with the assistant manager.

Test your understanding 4

Ensure that the following information is included:

(a)   the full name and title of the person(s) you intend or are required to meet

(b)   the full and precise name and address of the relevant organisation

(c)   the telephone number of the organisation together with the area code and the extension of the person you must see

(d)   the time, date and anticipated length of the meeting

(e)   the exact location of the meeting (e.g. which room on which floor in which block)

(f)   outline details of the matter to be discussed

(g)   travel directions and details of entrance points and security procedures.

It is, of course, equally important for those details to be sent to people who may be intending to visit you.

Test your understanding 5

C

Contact the supervisor immediately and explain the problem. Terri should suggest that the most urgent task is completed first before starting one of the others.

The role of information

Introduction

This chapter identifies the role that information plays in the work of the finance function, before moving on to look at the importance of data and information security. This chapter considers some of the major risks to the security of manual and computerised systems and data, including cybersecurity, and discusses the controls available to reduce or eliminate these risks.

ASSESSMENT CRITERIA	CONTENTS
7.1 The role of information in the work of the finance function	1 Information in the work of the finance function
7.2 The importance of data and information security	2 The importance of data and information security

1 Information in the work of the finance function

1.1 Useful information

Information needs to be useful if it is to enable the finance function and other parts of the organisation to operate efficiently. If information is not useful, the time and cost incurred in preparing to the information will have been incurred for no benefit, and may even be detrimental if control and decision-making is based upon that information.

The characteristics of useful information are:

- comparable – this enables the users of information to make meaningful comparisons with equivalent information relating to a previous accounting period, a budget or forecast or a competitor.

- consistent – this relates to consistency in both the basis of calculation or estimation and in the presentation of the information.

- understandable – this relates to the method of presentation and classification of information, along with the language used. If information is not understood by the user then it will have no benefit, or worse, be misunderstood and be detrimental to decision-making and control.

- relevant and reliable – information is relevant if it is likely to affect the decision-making of the information user and is reliable if it has been calculated or estimated in an appropriate manner.

- timely – information is timely if it is available when required for the purposes of control and decision-making in the organisation.

To illustrate the characteristics noted, consider the annual plant and equipment depreciation charge for an organisation. Normally, a consistent accounting policy for calculating the annual depreciation charge is adopted e.g. 20% per annum using the straight-line basis.

Calculating depreciation consistently will also make it easier to compare the depreciation expense year-on-year.

Checking the calculations and application of any assumptions made would help to confirm their accuracy and reliability.

Understandability could be improved by providing written explanations of the method and rate of depreciation used. Depending upon who the user of that information is, the amount of detail, and the wording used should reflect the needs of that specific user. For example, if supplying information to a colleague in the finance function, technical language and little explanation may be required as they will understand the subject matter. However, if supplying the information to a non-financial person (such as a production manager), it may require additional explanation, avoiding technical language or jargon as far as possible.

Finally, information must be available when it is needed to help managers with control and decision-making – it must be timely.

Of course, estimates such as the useful life of plant and equipment may need to be revised over time in order to ensure that the information remains relevant and reliable. Such a change might impact on the users' understanding and the comparability of the information over different time periods. We will need to address this issue by ensuring appropriate communication of the change and its implications for the depreciation charge recognised.

1.2 The use of digital technologies

The use of digital technologies to collect, process and disseminate data and information is increasingly common in most organisations, irrespective of their size. Even the smallest organisation may use laptops, tablets and hand-held devices to capture, process and classify financial data into useful information, but the nature, extent and sophistication of digital technologies used will depend on numerous factors including the nature of the business's activity, the data available and the size and resources of the organisation.

The advantages of digital capture, processing, storage and dissemination of data include:

- reduced operational costs

- human error is reduced, improving the quality of data

- rapid and easy capture of data

- improved security of data

- improved ease of access to those requiring the data, including multiple or remote users

- improved ability to track and analyse data resulting in improved management and control

- environmental and commercial benefits from using less paper, saving on purchase and storage costs whilst also reducing the adverse impact on the environment resulting from paper manufacturing, storage and disposal.

The disadvantages of digital data capture include:

- the capital cost of acquiring or developing the software, apps or acquiring the licences required. As the use of these technologies becomes more common these costs are falling particular where organisations use 'off-the-shelf' technologies.

- staff training costs and competencies required to use and understand the processes involved

- reliance upon systems that may crash or be unavailable for any reason, particularly if staff do not have the underpinning knowledge and understanding of systems and processes to recreate information manually

- security of data may be compromised by e.g. hackers or corrupted software

- loss or inadequacy of tracking and analytical capability to meet user needs.

Many organisations use hand-held devices to record the initial receipt of inventory from a supplier, and its movement during the manufacturing stage through to the despatch to the customer. Frequently, customers are asked to sign for receipt of goods on a hand-held electronic device. Retailers, in particular, make use of such technology as members of staff can advise customers of the availability of specific items, or whether it can be sourced from another location.

Digital technology is used by a range of organisations in a number of ways.

- M&S have trialled an in-queue checkout with a member of staff using a hand-held device to scan purchases and take card payment to speed up the process of customers paying for purchases.

- Ikea has in-store touchscreens for customers to access product details, availability and ordering.

- Nike's 'Speed Shop' which enables online ordering and reserving, accessing the product via an in-store locker using the customer's smartphone to access the product selected and then try on and, if purchased, take payment without interaction with anyone else.

- Ocado's business model fundamentally depends upon customers being able to order goods online, make payment, have delivery to a nominated address and book a delivery slot.

- Amazon Fresh in high street locations enables users of the Amazon app to select goods off-the-shelf and payment is automatically deducted via the app without the need to queue or pay for the goods at a till.

- Audi has a 'build your car' facility within its website that customers can use to review and choose the model and customisation of a car purchase.

- Many service providers, such as dentists, opticians and general practitioners have online booking and treatment recording services.

- Accountants use 'data analytic' software, allowing them to import data from a client's finance system and analyse it to identify unusual (and hence risky) transactions or balances and investigate those that are most significant to the client's financial statements.

1.3 Cloud accounting

 Definition

Cloud accounting is an accounting system that is accessed through the internet. This contrasts with desktop-based systems which require regular software updates and back-up procedures.

Advantages of cloud accounting include:

- the ability to access data anywhere and at any time from multiple locations

- access to real-time information, rather than having to wait for processing and output

- always uses the latest version of software

- the functionality to use analytical tools, either within the cloud accounting software itself, or provided via third party apps and tools

- the ability to grant secure access to data and information to trusted third parties e.g. the organisation's auditor or financial advisor

- connection to bank accounts to enable payments to be made e.g. periodic VAT payments, or to enable customers to pay for goods and services.

Disadvantages of cloud accounting include:

- reliance upon the speed and reliability of internet connections

- lack of customisation software so that only 'standard' packages are available which may not precisely meet the needs of the organisation

- lack of data security, particularly if it contains information that is regarded as confidential or sensitive, such as the personal details of customers and bank account information

- 'lock-in' to one system which may prevent or deter transfer to another provider of cloud accounting services.

To overcome some of the limitations above, some cloud accounting systems have developed to such an extent that they meet the niche or particular needs of different types of business, such as freelance workers, retailers and service providers. They are often integrated so that, for example, customer receipts are matched against invoices, and the receivables' ledger and ledger control account are also updated, reducing transaction recording time whilst also performing the control account reconciliation.

1.4 Information and documentation received by the finance function

The finance function **receives** a broad range of information and documentation from different parts of the business. It may be expressed in both financial and non-financial terms. The finance function must be able to understand, record, summarise and classify that information and documentation in a number of ways.

Budgetary information may be received from other parts of the business, such as inventory control, production, sales and despatch. It may be that the finance function has requested information from the various departments, perhaps on standardised documentation to initiate and progress the budget preparation and approval process.

For example, inventory control may quantify the amount of available storage capacity it has (or it needs) to cope with changes in production. The finance function may need to recognise costs for any additional storage capacity required. The production department may quantify the requirements for materials and components and the finance function will then need to convert this information into a financial or budgetary requirement. Usually, it is the finance function that coordinates and aggregates the various departmental budgets into a single document expressed in financial terms, ensuring that it is coherent and consistent.

Inventory control includes the receipt of materials, components and goods from suppliers, their storage and location and their subsequent issue to other departments e.g. production or despatch. The finance function will receive notification from inventory control that goods were received, specifying the date of receipt, the quantity and description of goods received (perhaps sending the goods received note). The finance function can then use this information to record the receipt of goods as an expense and as a liability and match it with purchase orders and invoices.

Costing information may comprise the quantity of products produced within a specified period of time. This will often be quite detailed when a business produces a range of products to different specifications or requirements. The finance function may use this information to produce the costings required, such as the total cost, perhaps split between fixed and variable components. This information could then be used to assist with pricing decisions.

Information from suppliers normally includes:

- goods received notes as evidence of the receipt of goods which is the point at which we should recognise that an expense has been incurred, with a liability outstanding until it is settled

- invoices for goods and services received which will be used to update the accounting records

- credit notes from a supplier when goods have not been received or were returned, perhaps because they were damaged, which will be used to reduce the expense and associated liability

- statements of account to summarise invoices and amounts outstanding, which can be used to check against the relevant payables' ledger account to confirm that it is fairly stated, or to raise queries with the supplier.

Information from customers normally includes:

- orders for goods, which will be forwarded to the relevant department e.g. sales or inventory control, perhaps with prices added by the finance function

- signed despatch notes from customers to acknowledge that they have received goods, which can be used as a basis for raising a sales invoice

- requests for a credit note if goods were not received, or were returned, perhaps because they were unsuitable or damaged

- remittance advices to confirm which invoices have been paid by the customer, along with notification of the manner of payment e.g. accompanying cheque or by direct credit into the bank account.

1.5 Information and documentation produced by the finance function

The finance function **produces** a broad range of information and documentation for different parts of the business. The information is likely to be stated in both financial and non-financial terms. The finance function must be able to produce, record, summarise and classify that information and ensure that it is in a usable and understandable form for the intended users.

Budgetary information will normally be produced by the finance function. Often, the budgeting planning process will consist of the finance function requesting information from other parts of the business, such as inventory control, production, sales and despatch departments. Based upon this information, the finance function will then commence the budget preparation process. This is likely to involve regular communication with the other parts of the business to seek additional information or clarification of information previously submitted to ensure that any inconsistencies or problems are resolved.

Following preparation and approval of the budgets or forecasts, the finance function will often prepare regular reports to enable departments and the business as a whole to monitor performance and to assist decision-making and control by managers. The information produced could be, for example, monthly management accounts with variances between budget and actual performance highlighted so that attention can be focussed on the key issues.

Inventory control covers receipt of materials, components and goods from suppliers, their storage and location and their subsequent issue to other departments e.g. production. The finance function will record the receipt of goods as an expense and liability and match it with delivery notes and purchase invoices. Note that the flow of information may involve several business departments or functions, depending upon the size and complexity of the organisation.

Costing information may involve the calculation of standard costs to assist business decision-making. Costing information produced may also include the calculation of total cost per unit, perhaps split between fixed and variable costs to further assist business decision-making.

Information produced for suppliers normally includes:

- remittance advices to confirm the invoices and amounts paid, plus reference to the method of payment e.g. cheque or direct payment to the supplier's bank account

- requests for a credit note if goods were not received or were returned for any reason.

Information produced for customers normally includes:

- despatch notes for the customer to sign upon receipt of goods

- sales invoices

- credit notes when goods have not been delivered, were damaged in transit, or the wrong goods were supplied

- statements of account to confirm invoices and amounts due and/or overdue.

Other information produced by the finance function is likely to include:

- cash and petty cash books of prime entry, including supporting invoices, vouchers and receipts

- bank reconciliations and reconciliations of the petty cash balance

- list of cash and cheque receipts for banking

- summaries of the available cash balance to ensure that the organisation does not exceed its loan and overdraft facilities

- accounting transactions and ledger accounts as a basis for preparing periodic management accounting and financial accounting information

- summaries of wage and salary payments required each week or month, along with the related returns and payments to HMRC

- preparing information and returns required by HMRC to support payments of VAT and other business taxes.

2 The importance of data and information security

2.1 Security, privacy and confidentiality of information

 Definitions

Cybersecurity is the application of processes, systems and controls to protect systems, networks, programs, devices and data from cyberattacks.

A **cyberattack** is an attempt to damage or destroy a computer network or system.

What are the risks associated with data and information security?

1   **Physical intrusion** leading to theft or damage of assets. Theft includes loss and illegal copying.

2   **Physical damage** to hardware or computer media. This includes malicious damage, poor operating conditions, natural disasters and simple wear and tear, any of which can physically damage hardware and storage media such as disks, tapes and diskettes. This represents a triple threat – the cost of repair or replacement of hardware, the danger of damaged data or program files and the cost of computer down time.

The loss of accounting records could be sufficient to cause the company to fail. Most non-technical users of systems would be surprised that there is an inherent risk to any computer system. Systems failure can mean that data is lost, or physical damage can occur in a manner that is virtually impossible to guard against in a cost-effective way.

3   **Damage to data** – hackers, viruses, program bugs, hardware and media faults can all damage data files. The havoc caused by damaged data is made worse if it is not detected and rectified quickly. Hacking activities can:

- generate information which is of potential use to a competitor organisation

- provide the basis for fraudulent activity

- cause data corruption by the introduction of unauthorised computer programs and processing onto the system, otherwise known as 'computer viruses'

- alter or delete the files

- result in the infection of systems by ransomware, typically requiring a payment in crypto-currency to unlock the system. A famous example of this was the 'Wannacry' cyber attack in 2017. This had worldwide implications including the infection of NHS systems leading to the cancellation of operations and significant disruption.

4   **Operational mistakes** – due to non-deliberate events such as running the wrong program, or inadvertently deleting data that is still of value to the organisation – this can cause significant problems, ranging from the need to recover files and repeat computer processing runs, to the possibility of losing customers.

Links to the Internet bring extra security risks. Examples include the following:

- viruses can spread through the network

- disaffected employees can cause deliberate damage to data or systems

- hackers may be able to steal data or damage the system

- employees may download inaccurate information or imperfect or virus-ridden software from an external network

- information sent from one part of an organisation to another may be intercepted

- the communications link itself may break down.

Note that in the nuclear energy sector, critical safety and security systems are isolated from the internet because of the severe consequences which would result from the issues described above.

5 **Industrial espionage/fraud** – can lead to loss of confidentiality with sensitive information being obtained by outsiders or unauthorised employees. Industrial espionage and sabotage can yield significant advantages to competitors, and fraud and blackmail is a significant threat.

A significant amount of time, effort, cost and resource is used by many businesses to ensure that data and information is secure. Why is this?

- To protect data and information which is commercially sensitive and which, if available to competitors, would give them a competitive advantage.

- To support efficient and effective ways of working and using the data and information available to the business.

- To maintain the confidentiality of personal data and information, such as the home address, contact details and payroll-related information of individual employees.

- To maintain the confidentiality of information from customers and suppliers, such as bank account details which, if available to others, could be open to inappropriate use.

- To ensure the completeness and reliability of data and information by minimising the risk of inappropriate access and amendment.

- To ensure compliance with legal and regulatory requirements regarding data handling, storage, use and transfer to others, such as the following UK examples:

    - General Data Protection Regulation (GDPR) 2016

    - Computer Misuse Act 1990 dealing with inappropriate use of computers

    - Data Protection Act 2018 dealing with how personal data is stored, protected, amended or deleted.

    In doing so, fines, penalties and adverse publicity are avoided.

For data and information regarded as private and confidential, it is important that it is accessed and used only for appropriate purposes by suitably trained and trusted individuals. Individuals working in the finance function (including payroll) often have in-house training to emphasise the importance of confidentiality and appropriate use of data and information.

The inappropriate use of confidential data and information may also be covered in contracts of employment. Deliberate or accidental misuse or disclosure of such information may result in the employee being subject to disciplinary action, including dismissal.

For example, employees who process payroll information may have access to the personal data of colleagues. They should only access that personal data for legitimate purposes (to assist with the processing of payroll payments and supporting records) and not for any other purposes, such as personal curiosity or to disclose that information to another without appropriate justification.

An unjustified breach of privacy and confidentiality may lead to the organisation being exposed to legal action for breach of civil or criminal law. An employee whose information was inappropriately accessed, used or disclosed could sue for breach of confidentiality or for negligence and receive financial compensation for the breach. Reference has already been made to GDPR and the criminal penalties that may be imposed for breach of that regulation.

2.2 Security measures

Data security is always important, irrespective of whether the business uses computerised or manual systems and processes. For example, inappropriate access to computer files containing supplier and customer contact and bank details is no different if the same information were accessed in a manual system, such as a supplier details list or bank account payment details.

Data security can be divided into a number of separate functions:

- **Threat avoidance:** this might mean changing the design of the system.

- **Prevention:** it is practically impossible to prevent all threats in a cost-effective manner, but those threats can be minimised.

- **Deterrence:** the system should try to both prevent unauthorised access and deter people from trying to access the system. Computer controls to prevent and detect access include passwords and hardware keys. As an example of a possible deterrent, computer misuse by employees could be treated as grounds for disciplinary action or dismissal. Similarly, in a manual system, a book of supplier contact and bank account details could be kept under the personal control of a senior member of the accounts department, with a requirement that it is stored in a locked drawer, cupboard or safe unless required.

- **Detection:** if the system is accessed without authorisation, there should be controls to detect that this has occurred and report it to the appropriate personnel. Detection techniques are often combined with prevention techniques. Computer controls will therefore include control logs of unauthorised attempts to gain access and manual reviews of amendments made to program and data files.

- **Recovery:** if data security has been compromised, its consequences should be limited as far as possible. Procedures should be in place to ensure that if the computer system was destroyed or compromised by a virus, then processing could resume quickly. A basic control procedure would be a complete, and regular, backup of all data. Businesses also often have a formal 'disaster recovery' plan in place for such eventualities.

- **Correction:** any unauthorised changes made to computer systems should be corrected as soon as possible. This means that complete backups of all data are available and that staff are properly trained in the procedures necessary for recovery and re-installation of data in an emergency situation.

2.3 Physical security

Physical security includes protection against natural and man-made disaster, e.g. fire, flood, etc. Examples of measures to avoid physical damage to the system include:

- fire precautions, e.g. smoke and heat detectors, training for staff in observing safety procedures and alarms, fire suppression systems (such as inert gas systems to protect computer hardware)

- devices to protect against power surges

- appropriate positioning of computer hardware away from sources of heat and damp

- the use of air-conditioning to maintain temperatures at safe levels.

Physical security also includes protection against intruders and theft. As computers and other hardware become smaller and more portable, they are at greater risk of theft. This applies equally to manual systems and documents which could easily be stolen, scanned or photographed, perhaps by a mobile phone.

Burglar alarms should be installed and a log of all equipment maintained. Employees with authorised access to the equipment and documents who are taking it off-site should book it out. They should also ensure that they have adequate security whilst in transit or at home or a third-party location. It would not be the first (or last) time that loss or damage to equipment or documents has occurred in such circumstances – for example in January 2009 a health worker lost a memory stick containing the medical details of 6,000 prisoners at HMP Preston. The data was encrypted and password protected but the password had been written on a note attached to the stick!

Security guards, closed circuit TV monitoring access or other mechanical devices such as door locks and electronic devices, e.g. badge readers and card entry systems, may control access to buildings. Even within a building, authorised access to certain parts of the building may be further restricted by the use of keypads, swipe cards etc. for example to access the payroll or HR departments.

2.4   Data security

Guidelines for data security include keeping files and documents in fireproof cabinets, shredding computer printouts and documents after use if they include confidential information, controlling access to data, (e.g. passwords and physical access controls) and taking back-ups of data to minimise the risks of destruction or alteration.

To offset the risk of fraudulent attacks there must be:

- adequate control over input/processing/programs

- strict division or segregation of duties to ensure that one individual is not solely responsible for recording the full cycle of a transaction

- regular internal audit review of systems and controls to ensure that controls operate effectively.

Good data security procedures help to maintain the confidentiality of information from customers and suppliers, such as bank account details which, if available to others, could be open to abuse.

To avoid breach of confidentiality, there should be controls over input and output. With online systems there should be individual passwords issued only to authorised personnel, restricted access to files at the terminals and a computer log of attempted violations.

All disks containing important information must be backed up on a regular basis. Information on a computer is vulnerable: hard disks and computer systems can fail, viruses can wipe a disk, careless operators can delete files and very careless operators can delete whole areas of a hard disk by mistake. Computers can also be damaged or stolen. For these reasons backing up of data is essential. This involves making copies of essential files, together with necessary update transactions, and keeping them on another computer, or on some form of storage media so that copies can be recreated (In modern cloud-based systems this happens automatically in real-time). Master file copies should be taken at regular intervals and kept at locations away from the main computer installation.

Contingency plans for a disaster should include standby facilities, with a similar computer user or a bureau facility to allow processing to continue.

2.5 Rules for using passwords

If passwords are used for authentication in a computer system, the following rules should be observed:

- It must not be possible to guess the password easily, such as the use of names, motor vehicle licence numbers, birth dates or similar.

- The password should consist of at least one non-letter character (special character or number) and have at least six characters. The selection of trivial passwords (BBBBBB, 123456, Password) must be prevented.

- Preset passwords (e.g. set by the manufacturer at the time of delivery) must be changed to individually selected, unique passwords as soon as possible.

- The password must be kept secret and should be known only to the authorised user. It must not be written down.

- The password must be changed regularly, e.g. every 90 days. This will ensure that if an unauthorised person has obtained it, he or she will have limited use.

- The password should be altered if it has, or may have, come to the knowledge of unauthorised persons.

- After any alteration of the password, previous passwords should no longer be used and re-use of previous passwords should be prevented by the IT system.

 Test your understanding 1

You have been asked for suggestions for a checklist of control procedures to remind authorised users about password security in the IT department.

What suggestions would you make?

2.6 Controls to help prevent hacking

 Definition

Hacking is an attempt to exploit a computer network or private network. It represents unauthorised access to a system for an illicit purpose. It may be done with the intention of committing fraud or another illegal activity, or perhaps only for the 'challenge' of being able to do it; in either situation, the consequences can be just as damaging.

Once hackers have gained access to the system, there are several damaging options available to them. For example, they may:

- gain access to the file that holds all of the system ID codes, passwords and authorisations

- discover the method used for generating/authorising passwords

- discover maintenance codes, which would render the system easily accessible.

By specifically identifying the risks that the hacker represents, controls can be designed that will help to prevent such activity occurring. Examples include:

- **Physical security** – check that terminals and PCs are kept under lock and key and ensure that, where dial-in communication links are in place, a call-back facility is used. (In call-back, the person dialling in must request that the system calls them back to make the connection).

- **Authorisation** – Management often requires that the contents of certain files (e.g. payroll) remain confidential and are only available to authorised staff. This may be achieved by keeping removable disks containing the files in a locked cabinet and issuing them only for authorised use.

- **Passwords** – the controls over passwords must be stringently enforced and password misuse should represent a serious disciplinary offence within an organisation. Associated with the password is a list of files, and data within files, which the user is allowed to inspect. Attempts to access unauthorised files or data will be prohibited by the operating system and reported. For example, an order clerk would be allowed access to a stock file, but not employee files. Similarly, the clerk would be allowed access to customer files for the purpose of recording an order, but would not necessarily be able to inspect details of the account. For systems that use passwords and logging on techniques, the workstation should not be left in the middle of editing. A screensaver with password control can be used for short absences, which avoids closing down the machine.

- **Data encryption** – files can be encrypted to render them unintelligible unless a decoding password is supplied. Data may be coded so that it is not understandable to any casual observer who does not have access to suitable decryption software. Encryption provides a double benefit. It protects against people gaining access to the system, and it protects against the tapping (monitoring network traffic) of data whilst being transmitted from one machine to another.

- **System logs** – every activity on a system should be logged and subject to some form of exception reporting, e.g. unusual dates or times of access could be reported.

- **Random checks** – the 'constable on the beat' approach checks who is doing what at random intervals on the system and ensures that they are authorised to perform those activities.

- **Shielding of (Video Display Units) VDUs** – to protect against people with detection equipment being able to view remotely what is being displayed on VDUs, the units may be shielded to prevent the transmission of radiation that can be detected.

2.7 Preventative steps against computer viruses

It is extremely difficult to guard against the introduction of computer viruses. Even seemingly harmless screen savers have been known to contain deadly viruses that destroy computer systems. You should not download from the Internet or open emails that have attachments, unless you know the source of the email and you trust that source. If you are in doubt you should ask your line manager or IT department for permission to open documents or attachments.

Steps may be taken to control the introduction and spread of viruses, but these will usually only be effective in controlling the spread of viruses by well-meaning individuals. The actions of hackers or malicious employees are less easy to control.

Preventative steps may include:

- Anti-virus software to prevent corruption of the system by viruses. However, the focus of the program is to detect and cure known viruses, and therefore it will not always restore data or software that has been corrupted by the virus. As new viruses are being detected almost daily, it is virtually impossible for the virus detection software to be effective against all viruses – anti-virus software must therefore be kept up-to-date

- Control over the use of external software (e.g. checked for viruses before use) and approved by the IT department

- Use of only tested, marked disks/memory sticks within the organisation

- Restricted access to CDs & flash drives on all PCs/workstations

- Passwords and user numbers can be used to limit the opportunities for unauthorised people to access the system via the public communications network.

3 Summary

This chapter focussed on the role of information in the work of the finance function. It also considered the importance of data and information security, including cyber security, and how data and information may be at risk and how it can be protected.

Test your understanding answers

Test your understanding 1

Some of the suggestions that would be included in a checklist for password security are:

- Passwords are meant to be secret and not revealed to anyone else.

- Never write it down.

- Change your password regularly or if you suspect someone knows it.

- Do not choose an obvious password such as your name, or in the case of a PIN, your date or year of birth.

- Try to avoid onlookers seeing you key in your password.

- For keyboard passwords, choose keys that require both hands rather than one or two finger, easy runs along a pattern of the keys (e.g. QWERTY).

KAPLAN PUBLISHING

MOCK ASSESSMENT

1 Mock Assessment Questions

Task 1 (10 marks)

This task is about different business types and their functions.

This task contains parts (a) to (c).

(a) Identify whether the following statements about business ownership are true or false. (3 marks)

Statement	True ✓	False ✓
A sole trader cannot have employees.		
Owners of a limited company will always have the right to participate in the day-to-day running of the company.		
A partnership must have a written agreement which details the rights and responsibilities of the partners to each other.		

You work for a team of professional business advisors and have been asked to contribute to a brochure which provides information on the different types of business entity. The brochure will include a checklist of the characteristics of different types of business.

(b) Identify the correct characteristics that relate to the relevant business type. There may be more than one characteristic relevant to each business type. (5 marks)

Characteristic	Sole trader ✓	Partnership ✓	Limited company ✓
This business type can be established informally without the need for a formal procedure.			
This business type is not a separate entity distinct from its owners.			
This business type separates ownership from the management of the business.			

A firm of accountants has decided to open an office in a new country. This will require the installation of a new information management system and additional staff.

(c) Identify which functions of the business would have responsibility for each of the following tasks. (2 marks)

Task	Business function
Selection of the information management system for the new office	Option 1
Ensuring that the new office complies with local business regulations	Option 2

Option 1	Option 2
Human resources	Business operations
Information technology and finance	Production

Task 2   **(13 marks)**

This task is about the finance function, its information requirements and sources, and its role within the wider organisation.

This task contains parts (a) to (c).

Julie has recently joined the accounting department of MM. Julie has some relevant accounting experience from her previous job, but will not be familiar with MM's processes. Initially, Julie will have responsibility for recording petty cash transactions and for ensuring that there will be adequate stationery supplies available to colleagues in the accounts department. Julie will also deal with other ad hoc duties as she becomes familiar with the work of her colleagues in the accounts department.

As Julie is due to start work next week, you have been asked to provide some notes to help her settle into her role. You have decided the notes should start with the main roles of the finance function.

(a) **From the list below, identify the FOUR main roles of the finance function at MM by placing them into your notes.** (4 marks)

List of roles:

Ensuring the security of the manufacturing processes
Ensuring the confidentiality of accounting information
Managing staff in other internal departments
Ensuring the reliability of financial data
Producing statutory financial statements
Providing accounting information to other internal departments
Providing systems support to other departments

Notes for Julie **Main roles of the finance function:**

It is now Julie's first week at MM and you are helping with her induction into the organisation. You have been asked to highlight important policies and procedures on MM's intranet that Julie should familiarise herself with.

(b) From the list below, identify FIVE policies or procedures Julie should familiarise herself with by placing them into your notes.

(5 marks)

List of policies and procedures:

Annual leave entitlement policy
Research and development policy
Sales team selling targets
Sickness and absence reporting
Vehicle maintenance checking procedures
Warehouse despatch procedures
Accounts department study leave policy
Ethics and confidentiality of information policy
Stationery ordering procedures for the accounts department

Notes for Julie   **Policies and procedures you need to be familiar with:**

Julie has been working with you for a few months now and you are aware of some concerns in relation to her performance. During meetings, Julie appears uninterested and does not participate. There have also been instances of Julie misunderstanding instructions and not meeting deadlines. You decide to help Julie to develop the skills which are important in her role.

(c) **Identify FOUR ways Julie could develop the necessary skills to help her in her role** (4 marks)

Ways for Julie to develop her skills	✓
Prepare for meetings by thinking of relevant issues in advance to raise and discuss.	
Work on your own and don't ask for help or guidance.	
Identify the speaker at meetings so that you can develop a network of colleagues and work contacts.	
Take your mobile phone into meetings and set it to silent mode to text friends who are difficult to contact as they have limited free time.	
Wait until the person speaking has finished before asking questions.	
Take notes at meetings so that you can remember what was discussed and any decisions made.	
Interrupt the speaker during meetings to ask questions.	

Task 3 (14 marks)

This task is about corporate social responsibility (CSR), ethics and sustainability.

This task contains parts (a) to (c).

MM has recently committed itself to improving its Corporate Social Responsibility (CSR) activities. You are part of a team asked to prepare a staff summary of the benefits of positive Corporate Social Responsibility, and identify CSR initiatives that staff could have involvement with.

(a) **Complete the two sections of the staff summary, by choosing THREE benefits to MM of having a positive attitude to CSR and THREE CSR initiatives to raise local community awareness that employees could have involvement with.** (6 marks)

Possible benefits of CSR to MM (choose THREE):

Producing more products will mean using more resources even if good CSR practices are introduced.
CSR will help to improve the reputation of the organisation.
CSR will help to attract and retain staff.
There will be some costs incurred in order to introduce CSR initiatives into the organisation.
CSR will help to reduce costs associated with wastage and inefficiency.
Professional consultants will need to be hired to provide staff with appropriate training and awareness of CSR.

Possible CSR initiatives to raise local community awareness (choose THREE):

MM could donate surplus or waste resources, such as paper and cardboard, to a local nursery for use by children in play activities.
MM could change its manufacturing and production processes.
MM could permit members of staff to have leave of absence from work to act as a volunteer in a local charity.
Offering staff training and supporting those wishing to gain further qualifications.
MM could sponsor members of staff who undertake fund-raising activities for a local charity.
MM could try to ensure that all staff minimise costs and expenses to the organisation.

MM Manufacturing
Staff Summary
Corporate Social Responsibility

Benefits of CSR to MM Manufacturing.
CSR initiatives to raise community awareness.

(b) Which of the following TWO are NOT fundamental ethical principles? (2 marks)

	✓
Confidentiality	
Independence	
Integrity	
Neutrality	
Professional behaviour	

(c) Categorise the following safeguards according to whether they are created by the profession, or are present in the work environment. **(6 marks)**

Safeguard	Profession ✓	Work environment ✓
Continuing professional development		
Professional standards		
Quality controls		
Rotation of personnel		
Corporate governance regulations		
Appointment of an ethics officer		

Task 4 (22 marks)

This task is about processing bookkeeping transactions and communicating information.

This task contains parts (a) to (g).

MM has supplied goods to Premier Products Ltd. You have been asked to complete the invoice by calculating the invoice amounts.

(a) Refer to the price list and complete the FOUR boxes in the invoice below. **(4 marks)**

Price List:

Product code	Price each (£)
ADA14	5.50
BDA14	6.00
BDA16	3.50
CDE24	2.40
DOX18	9.00
DOX28	9.50

Invoice:

MM Manufacturing
5 Liverpool Way
Brayton, BA42 5YZ
VAT Registration No. 983 3624 07
Invoice No. 2178

To:

Premier Products Ltd

121 Old Road

Grungetown, GR78 9DR

Invoice date: 12 June 20X6

Delivery date: 12 June 20X6

Customer account code: PP007

Quantity of units	Product code	Price each (£)	Net amount (£)	VAT amount (£)	Total amount (£)
65	CDE24				

Terms of payment: Net monthly account

Your next task is to enter the invoice into the appropriate daybook.

(b) Record the invoice in the correct daybook by:

- **selecting the correct daybook title, and**

- **making the necessary entries.**   **(6 marks)**

∇ Drop down lists for task 4 (b):

Cash book	Premier Products Ltd
Discounts allowed daybook	MM Manufacturing
Discounts received daybook	
Petty cash book	
Purchases daybook	
Purchases returns daybook	
Sales daybook	
Sales returns daybook	

Date 20X6	Details	Account code	Invoice number	Total (£)	VAT (£)	Net (£)
▽						
12 June	▽		2178			

MM Manufacturing is considering offering its customers a 5.0% prompt payment discount for payment within ten days of the date of invoice.

(c) **Calculate the amount that Premier Products Ltd would deduct if a 5.0% prompt discount was offered on the invoice in (a) and the invoice paid within ten days.** (1 mark)

£ _____

(d) **What is the latest date by which MM should receive the payment from Premier Products Ltd if the prompt payment discount was taken?** (1 mark)

▽ Drop down list for task 4 (d):

12 June 20X6
17 June 20X6
21 June 20X6
22 June 20X6
12 July 20X6

▽

The list of balances in the receivables ledger of MM shows the account of Louise & Partners has a credit balance of £358 which arose as a result of the customer making two payments to MM.

(e) Prepare a brief letter to be sent to Mr Browne at Louise Partners, explaining their overpayment and stating that a cheque is enclosed to clear the balance.

Note: Address details are not required and you can finish the letter with your job title, Accounts Assistant. (4 marks)

It is now early September and you are in the process of preparing MMs' payables ledger control account as at 31 August, as shown below.

Payables ledger control

Details	Amount (£)		Detail	Amount (£)
Bank	44,214		Balance b/f	78,954

You now have the totals of the purchases, discounts received and purchases returns daybooks and must record the appropriate amounts in the payables ledger control account.

Purchases daybook extract

Date 20X6	Details	Total (£)	VAT (£)	Net (£)
31 Aug	Totals	31,572	5,262	26,310

Discounts received daybook extract

Date 20X6	Details	Total (£)	VAT (£)	Net (£)
31 Aug	Totals	1,350	225	1,125

Purchases returns daybook extract

Date 20X6	Details	Total (£)	VAT (£)	Net (£)
31 Aug	Totals	600	100	500

(f) What will be the entries in the payables ledger control account?
(4 marks)

Tick whether each amount will be a debit or credit entry to the payables ledger control account.

Balances	Amount (£)	Debit ✓	Credit ✓
Entry from the purchases daybook			
Entry from the discounts received daybook			
Entry from the purchases returns daybook			

(g) What will be the balance carried down on the payables ledger control account?
(2 marks)

Amount (£)	Debit ✓	Credit ✓

Task 5
(10 marks)

This task is about control accounts, reconciliations and using journals to correct accounts.

This task contains parts (a) to (g).

You are required to reconcile the receivables ledger with the receivables ledger control account as at 31 August. These are the balances in the receivables ledger on 31 August.

Credit customers	Balances	
	Amount (£)	Debit/Credit
Baikal	15,987	Debit
Eerie	14,628	Debit
Louise & Partners	358	Credit
Michigan plc	17,242	Debit
Superior Ltd	11,746	Debit
Windermere	23,255	Debit

(a) If the receivables ledger control account agrees to the receivables ledger what will be the balance? **(2 marks)**

Amount (£)	Debit	Credit

The balance of the receivables ledger control account is £82,130

(b) What is the difference between the receivables ledger control account and the receivables ledger? **(1 mark)**

Amount (£)

Your manager wants to know what may have caused the difference shown in the reconciliation statement.

(c) Which TWO of the reasons below could NOT explain the difference you calculated in (b) above? **(2 marks)**

Reasons	✓
A credit note was entered twice in the receivables ledger control account.	
An invoice was entered twice in a customer ledger account in the receivables ledger.	
A receipt was entered twice in a customer ledger account in the receivables ledger.	
A discount allowed was entered twice in the receivables ledger control account.	
An invoice was entered twice in the receivables ledger control account.	
A discount allowed was not entered in a customer ledger account in the receivables ledger.	

You now move on to deal with some bank and cash issues.

(d) Which TWO of the following four items could require an entry in the cash book? **(2 marks)**

	✓
Bank charges	
Cheques not presented	
A direct debit	
Deposits not credited	

Mock Assessment Questions

You know that your colleague has correctly completed a reconciliation of the bank balance in the general ledger to the balance on the bank statement.

The general ledger balance at the end of September shows a credit balance of £2,358. The bank statement balance shows a debit balance of £1,053. The difference between the two balances is explained by unpresented cheques and uncleared lodgements.

(e) **How should the bank balance be reported in the final accounts?**

(1 mark)

As a current asset of £1,053	
As a current liability of £1,053	
As a current asset of £2,358	
As a current liability of £2,358	

Z Ltd has produced its year-end trial balance and has identified the following error:

An invoice for a motor vehicle repair of £240 was posted to the building repairs account.

(f) **Identify what type of error this is** **(1 mark)**

Error type	
Error of omission	
Error of principle	
Error of commission	
Reversal of entries	

(g) **Identify the impact on the suspense account to correct this error**

(1 mark)

Account	Debit	Credit	No impact
Suspense account			

176

KAPLAN PUBLISHING

Task 6 (7 marks)

This task is about the principles of contract law.

This task contains tasks (a) to (b)

(a) **Which one of the following is the highest ranking court in the UK?** **(1 mark)**

Court	✓
Court of Appeal	
The Supreme Court	
High Court of Justice	

Hilary advertised a printing press in a specialist trade journal for £15,000. Eleanor wrote to Hilary offering to buy it for £10,000. Hilary replied by return of post saying she would accept £13,000. When she heard nothing further from Eleanor, Hilary wrote again saying she would accept £10,000.

(b) **(i)** **Identify whether each of the following statements are true or false.** **(2 marks)**

Statement	True ✓	False ✓
An offer cannot be made to the whole world.		
The advert in the trade journal is an offer.		

(ii) **Identify whether each of the following statements are true or false.** **(2 marks)**

Statement	True ✓	False ✓
Eleanor's letter to Hilary is a counter offer.		
Hilary's first letter to Eleanor is a counter offer.		

(iii) **Identify whether each of the following statements are true or false** (2 marks)

Statement	True ✓	False ✓
The effect of a counter offer is to bring the original offer to an end.		
Hilary's second reply to Eleanor accepting £10,000 constitutes acceptance.		

Task 7 (10 marks)

This task is about bookkeeping systems, receipts and payments and the importance of information and data security.

This task contains tasks (a) to (d).

Max is a driving instructor who provides tuition to learners of all ages throughout the day and during some evenings. As Max travels regularly from one lesson to another, an assistant, Kim, has been hired to arrange bookings etc. if Max is not available.

Max has set up a cloud-based system on a mobile phone. The mobile phone contract enables Max to divert calls to Kim and for Kim to receive bookings and payments in advance as this is required to secure all bookings.

Max uses an accounting app to raise invoices for lessons when payment is received. All receipts from learners are paid into a business bank account, which Max can manage with an app on the mobile phone.

Max is able to transfer cash from the business bank account to a personal account to meet personal expenses. The accounting app is used to record the amount transferred from the business bank account to the personal account.

(a) **Identify THREE ways in which Max is benefitting from the use of digital technology.** **(3 marks)**

Max stores learners' personal contact details, such as name, address, phone number and email address on a personal laptop spreadsheet. The laptop password is 123ABC, which has not been changed for five years. Max regularly reminds Kim of the password as Kim also needs access to information stored on the laptop. Both Max and Kim have a paper note of the password in a kitchen drawer in their respective homes.

(b) **Identify which TWO of the following statements are true.**

(2 marks)

Statement	✓
Max is rarely in one place for more than two hours at a time, so there is no need to worry about data protection issues.	
Both the laptop and the spreadsheet should be protected by a separate password.	
It is acceptable not to change the laptop password as only two people use it.	
Max should not assume that learners automatically give their consent to the transfer of their personal data to other businesses so that pupils can be contacted regarding the availability of other goods and services.	

Sam uses a cloud-based accounting system and has received an alert that the bank statement has not reconciled. Payments were allocated correctly to purchase invoices, with one exception as follows:

- The invoice was for a professional subscription, which is exempt from VAT. The value of the invoice was £250 which Sam paid early to receive a 10% prompt payment discount, and therefore paid only £225.

(c) **Explain what action Sam should now take.** **(2 marks)**

(d) **State THREE ways in which the use of cloud-based accounting has been useful to Sam in this scenario.** **(3 marks)**

Task 8   **(14 marks)**

This task is about the external business environment.

This task contains parts (a) to (g).

(a) Identify TWO of the following items that explain why demand changes in response to changes in prices.   **(2 marks)**

	✓
Substitution effect	
Inflationary effect	
Deflationary effect	
Supply effect	
Income effect	

(b) Identify which ONE of the following situations is likely to cause a decrease in demand.   **(1 mark)**

Situation	✓
A decease in the price of a complementary product	
An increase in direct taxation on individuals	
An increase in population size	
Supply effect	
Income effect	

(c) Identify whether the following statements about supply are true or false.   **(3 marks)**

Statement	True ✓	False ✓
An increase in subsidies for manufacturers will increase supply.		
An increase in indirect taxes on prices (e.g. VAT) will increase supply.		
Technological improvements making production more efficient will increase supply.		

(d) Identify whether the following are examples of regressive or progressive taxation. **(3 marks)**

Statement	Regressive ✓	Progressive ✓
Individuals earning below a minimum income threshold suffer no taxes on income at all.		
VAT is charged at the same rate on essential foodstuffs to all customers and those on lower incomes spend a greater proportion of their income on these items.		
The rate of employee national insurance contributions falls from 12% to 2% above a certain level of income.		

Worldwide plc has recently signed a sales contract with a company based in the USA to supply 1,000 computer processor chips at a price of $100 each. Since signing the contract the exchange rate has changed from £1 = $1.30 to £1 = $1.20.

(e) Identify the statement which explains what has happened.

(1 mark)

	✓
The pound has appreciated against the US$.	
The US$ has depreciated against the pound.	
The pound has depreciated against the US$.	

(f) Identify which ONE of the following situations will occur due to the change in exchange rates. **(1 mark)**

Situation	✓
The sales proceeds in pounds will increase	
The sales proceeds in pounds will decrease	

(g)   Identify whether the following statements about interest rates
      are true or false.   (3 marks)

Statement	True ✓	False ✓
An increase in interest rates will encourage people to spend less and have a deflationary effect on prices.		
A decrease in interest rates will stimulate demand and have a positive effect on GDP growth.		
An increase in interest rates is beneficial to borrowers and detrimental to savers.		

KAPLAN PUBLISHING

2 Mock Assessment Answers

Task 1 (10 marks)

(a) Identify whether the following statements about business ownership are true or false. (3 marks)

Statement	True ✓	False ✓
A sole trader cannot have employees.		✓
Owners of a limited company will always have the right to participate in the day-to-day running of the company.		✓
A partnership must have a written agreement which details the rights and responsibilities of the partners to each other.		✓

(b) Identify the correct characteristics that relate to each of the business types noted below. There may be more than one characteristic relevant to each business type. (5 marks)

Characteristic	Sole trader	Partnership	Limited company
This business type can be established informally without the need for a formal procedure or documentation.	✓	✓	
This business type is not a separate entity distinct from its owners.	✓	✓	
This business type separates ownership and management of the business.			✓

(c) **Identify which functions of the business would have responsibility for each of the following tasks.**   (2 marks)

Task	Business function
Selection of the information management system for the new office	Information technology and finance
Ensuring that the new office complies with local business regulations	Business operations

Task 2   (13 marks)

(a)

> **Notes for Julie**
>
> **Main roles of the finance function:**
>
> Ensuring the confidentiality of accounting information
>
> Ensuring the reliability of financial data
>
> Producing statutory financial statements
>
> Providing accounting information to other internal departments

(b)

> **Notes for Julie**
>
> **Policies and Procedures you need to be familiar with:**
>
> Annual leave entitlement policy
>
> Sickness and absence reporting
>
> Accounts department study leave policy
>
> Ethics and confidentiality of information policy
>
> Stationery ordering procedures for the accounts department

(c)

Ways for Julie to develop her skills	✓
Prepare for meetings by thinking of relevant issues in advance to raise and discuss.	✓
Work on your own and don't ask for help or guidance.	
Identify the speaker at meetings so that you can develop a network of colleagues and work contacts.	✓

Take your mobile phone into meetings and set it to silent mode to text friends who are difficult to contact as they have limited free time.	
Wait until the person speaking has finished before asking questions.	✓
Take notes at meetings so that you can remember what was discussed and any decisions made.	✓
Interrupt the speaker to ask questions during meetings.	

Task 3 (14 marks)

(a) Complete the two sections of the staff summary, by choosing THREE benefits to MM of having a positive attitude to CSR and THREE CSR initiatives to raise local community awareness that employees could become involved with. (6 marks)

MM Manufacturing
Staff Summary
Corporate Social Responsibility
Benefits of CSR to MM CSR will help to improve the reputation of the organisation. CSR will help to attract and retain staff. CSR will help to reduce costs associated with wastage and inefficiency.
CSR initiatives to raise community awareness MM could donate surplus or waste resources, such as paper and cardboard, to a local nursery for use by children in play activities. MM could permit members of staff to have leave of absence from work to act as a volunteer in a local charity. MM could sponsor members of staff who undertake fund-raising activities for a local charity.

Tutorial note: Although some of the possible items listed may bring CSR benefits, the report requires you to identify those initiatives which are particularly relevant to the local community.

(b) Which of the following TWO are NOT fundamental ethical principles? **(2 marks)**

	✓
Confidentiality	
Independence	✓
Integrity	
Neutrality	✓
Professional behaviour	

(c) Categorise the following safeguards according to whether they are created by the profession, or are present in the work environment. **(6 marks)**

Safeguard	Profession ✓	Work environment ✓
Continuing professional development	✓	
Professional standards	✓	
Quality controls		✓
Rotation of personnel		✓
Corporate governance regulations	✓	
Appointment of an ethics officer		✓

Task 4 (22 marks)

(a) Refer to the price list and complete the FOUR boxes in the invoice below. (4 marks)

MM Manufacturing
5 Liverpool Way
Brayton, BA42 5YZ
VAT Registration No. 983 3624 07
Invoice No. 2178

To:	Invoice date: 12 June 20X6
Premier Products Ltd	Delivery date: 12 June 20X6
121 Old Road	Customer account code: PP007
Grungetown, GR78 9DR	

Quantity of units	Product code	Price each (£)	Net amount (£)	VAT amount (£)	Total amount (£)
65	CDE24	2.40	156.00	31.20	187.20

Terms of payment: Net monthly account

(b) Record the invoice in the correct daybook by:

- selecting the correct daybook title, and

- making the necessary entries. (6 marks)

Sales daybook ∇						
Date 20X6	Details	Account code	Invoice number	Total (£)	VAT (£)	Net (£)
12 June	Premier Products Ltd ∇	PP007	2178	187.20	31.20	156.00

(c) Calculate the amount that Premier Products Ltd would deduct if a 5.0% prompt discount was offered on the invoice in (a) and the invoice paid within ten days. (1 mark)

£	9.36

(d) What is the latest date by which MM should receive the payment from Premier Products Ltd if the prompt payment discount was taken? (1 mark)

22 June 20X6 ∇

(e) Prepare a brief letter to be sent to Mr Browne at Louise Partners, explaining their overpayment and stating that a cheque is enclosed to clear the balance.

Note: Address details are not required and you can finish the letter with your job title, Accounts Assistant. (4 marks)

> Dear Mr Browne,
>
> Our receivables ledger shows an erroneous overpayment recently made to MM Manufacturing has resulted in an amount of £358 owing to you.
>
> Please find enclosed a cheque for the amount due. If you require any further information relating to this payment, please contact me and I can provide supporting documentation and information.
>
> Yours sincerely,
>
> Accounts Assistant
>
> Enc.

(f) What will be the entries in the payables ledger control account? (4 marks)

Tick whether each amount will be debit or credit.

Balances	Amount (£)	Debit	Credit
Entry from the purchases daybook	31,572		✓
Entry from the discounts received daybook	1,350	✓	
Entry from the purchases returns daybook	600	✓	

(g) What will be the balance carried down on the payables ledger control account? (2 marks)

Amount (£)	Debit	Credit
64,362	✓	

Task 5   (10 marks)

(a) If the receivables ledger control account agrees to the receivables ledger what will be the balance?   (2 marks)

Amount (£)	Debit	Credit
82,500	✓	

(b) What is the difference between the receivables ledger control account and the receivables ledger?   (1 mark)

Amount (£)
370

(c) Which TWO of the reasons below could NOT explain the difference you calculated in (b) above?   (2 marks)

Reasons	✓
A credit note was entered twice in the receivables ledger control account.	
An invoice was entered twice in a customer ledger account in the receivables ledger.	
A receipt was entered twice in a customer ledger account in the receivables ledger.	✓
A discount allowed was entered twice in the receivables ledger control account.	
An invoice was entered twice in the receivables ledger control account.	✓
A discount allowed was not entered in a customer ledger account in the receivables ledger.	

(d) Which TWO of the following four items could require an entry in the cash book?   (2 marks)

Bank charges	✓
Cheques not presented	
A direct debit	✓
Deposits not credited	

An entry is required in the cash book for all correct items in the bank statement that have not yet been recorded in the cash book. These are the items that the business learns about when the bank statement has been received and should then record those items in its own accounting records i.e. initially in the cash book. Deposits not credited and cheques not presented have already been recorded in the cash book.

(e)   How should the bank balance be reported in the final accounts?

(1 mark)

As a current asset of £1,053	
As a current liability of £1,053	
As a current asset of £2,358	
As a current liability of £2,358	✓

The correct answer is a current liability of £2,358.

The corrected general ledger balance should be reported in the final accounts. In this case no other adjustments are needed to the general ledger balance as per the bank reconciliation. The reconciling items arise due to transactions being recorded at different times by the business and the bank. These may be referred to as 'timing differences'.

(f)   Identify what type of error this is

(1 mark)

Error type	
Error of omission	
Error of principle	
Error of commission	✓
Reversal of entries	

An error of commission is an error posted to the wrong account but it is the same nature of account that it should have been posted to i.e. both of these accounts are expense accounts.

(g)   Identify the impact on the suspense account to correct this error

(1 mark)

Account	Debit	Credit	No impact
Suspense account			✓

The correction of this error will not impact the suspense account. An error of commission does not cause the trial balance to not balance.

Task 6 (7 marks)

This task is about the principles of contract law.

This task contains tasks (a) to (b)

(a) **Which one of the following is the highest-ranking court in the UK?** **(1 mark)**

Court	✓
Court of Appeal	
The Supreme Court	✓
High Court of Justice	

(b) **(i)** **Identify whether each of the following statements are true or false.** **(2 marks)**

Statement	True ✓	False ✓
An offer cannot be made to the whole world.		✓
The advert in the trade journal is an offer.		✓

(ii) **Identify whether each of the following statements are true or false.** **(2 marks)**

Statement	True ✓	False ✓
Eleanor's letter to Hilary is a counter offer.		✓
Hilary's first letter to Eleanor is a counter offer.	✓	

(iii) **Identify whether each of the following statements are true or false.** **(2 marks)**

Statement	True ✓	False ✓
The effect of a counter offer is to bring the original offer to an end.	✓	
Hilary's second reply to Eleanor accepting £10,000 constitutes acceptance.		✓

Task 7 (10 marks)

(a) **Identify THREE ways in which Max is benefitting from the use of digital technology.** (3 marks)

> Examples of appropriate benefits include:
>
> Ease of access to financial information, particularly if working in different locations.
>
> Use of business banking app reduces the need to carry cash and/or debit/credit cards that could be lost or stolen.
>
> Learners pay in advance using the app or direct payment to minimise the risk of non-payment of fees.
>
> Sales and expenses are easily and quickly recorded using the business banking app.
>
> Flexibility of business activities which allow both Max and Kim to access relevant information when required.

(b) **Identify which of the following TWO statements are true.**
(2 marks)

Statement	✓
Max is rarely in one place for much more than two hours at a time, so there is no need to worry about data protection issues.	
Both the laptop and the spreadsheet should be protected by a separate password.	✓
It is acceptable not to change the laptop password as only two people use it.	
Max should not assume that pupils automatically give their consent to the transfer of their personal data to other businesses so that pupils can be contacted regarding the availability of other goods and services.	✓

(c) **Explain what action Sam should now take.** **(2 marks)**

> Sam should raise a credit note for the amount of the discount - £25.
>
> This will enable the bank payment to be reconciled with the subscription invoice and the credit note. Both the subscription invoice and credit note should be processed as a business expense.

(d) **State THREE ways in which the use of cloud-based accounting has been useful to Sam in this scenario.** **(3 marks)**

> Examples of appropriate comments include:
>
> Cash payments are automatically matched with invoices, which saves time processing transactions.
>
> Individual customer accounts are also updated automatically, which avoids the need to spend time reconciling the ledger control account with the total of individual ledger account balances.
>
> Any discrepancies are automatically highlighted, enabling Sam to focus time and attention where it is needed to resolve problems.

Task 8 (14 marks)

This task is about the external business environment.

(a) **Identify TWO of the following items that explain why demand changes in response to changes in prices.** **(2 marks)**

	✓
Substitution effect	✓
Inflationary effect	
Deflationary effect	
Supply effect	
Income effect	✓

(b) **Identify which ONE of the following situations is likely to cause a decrease in demand.** **(1 mark)**

Situation	✓
A decease in the price of a complementary product	
An increase in direct taxation on individuals	✓
An increase in population size	

(c) Identify whether the following statements about supply are true or false. **(3 marks)**

Statement	True ✓	False ✓
An increase in subsidies for manufacturers will increase supply.	✓	
An increase in indirect taxes on prices (e.g. VAT) will increase supply.		✓
Technological improvements making production more efficient will increase supply.	✓	

(d) Identify whether the following are examples of regressive or progressive taxation. **(3 marks)**

Statement	Regressive ✓	Progressive ✓
Individuals earning below a minimum income threshold suffer no taxes on income at all.		✓
VAT is charged at the same rate on essential foodstuffs to all customers and those on lower incomes spend a greater proportion of their income on these items.	✓	
The rate of employee national insurance contributions falls from 12% to 2% above a certain level of income.	✓	

Worldwide plc has recently signed a sales contract with a company based in the USA to supply 1,000 computer processor chips at a price of $100 each. Since signing the contract the exchange rate has changed from £1 = $1.30 to £1 = $1.20.

(e) Identify the statement which explains what has happened. **(1 mark)**

	✓
The pound has appreciated against the US$.	
The US$ has depreciated against the pound.	
The pound has depreciated against the US$.	✓

(f) Identify which ONE of the following situations will occur due to the change in exchange rates. **(1 mark)**

Situation	✓
The sales proceeds in pounds will increase	✓
The sales proceeds in pounds will decrease	

(g) Identify whether the following statements about interest rates are true or false. **(3 marks)**

Statement	True ✓	False ✓
An increase in interest rates will encourage people to spend less and have a deflationary effect on prices.	✓	
A decrease in interest rates will stimulate demand and have a positive effect on GDP growth.	✓	
An increase in interest rates is beneficial to borrowers and detrimental to savers.		✓

Appendix 1: Introduction to Bookkeeping

Introduction

This chapter recaps the key aspects of the Introduction to Bookkeeping unit.

UNIT LEARNING OBJECTIVES STILL RELEVANT FOR THE SYNOPTIC ASSESSMENT
LO1   Understand how to set up bookkeeping systems
LO2   Process customer transactions
LO3   Process supplier transactions

LO1 Understand how to set up bookkeeping systems

The purpose of business documents

- Initially a business transaction will take place; a credit sale, a credit purchase, a cash sale, a cash purchase, another expense either paid from the bank or by cash, cash paid into the bank, withdrawal of cash from the bank and owner's drawings.

- A **business document** will be produced e.g. an invoice.

- The transaction and details from the business document will be entered into the **books of prime entry**.

Business document	Purpose
Purchase order	A buyer generated document that authorises a purchase transaction.
Sales order	A seller generated document that authorises a sale to a customer, issued after the receipt of a purchase order.
Delivery note	A document accompanying goods despatched to a customer explaining what the delivery contains.
Goods received note	An internal document completed by the purchaser that records the details of goods received and contains similar information to a delivery note.
Invoice	A document that itemises a transaction between a buyer and a seller; it is a request for the buyer to make payment for goods sold or services provided by the seller.
Credit note	A document issued by a supplier to a customer cancelling part or all of a sales invoice.
Goods returned note	A document sent to the supplier by the customer detailing the goods returned and reason(s) for the return being made.
Remittance advice	A blank document that the customer completes when making a payment to the supplier. It shows the total payment being made and which invoices (less credit notes) the payment is paying off.

Statement of account	Customer:
	A statement that shows all the invoices and credit notes that have been sent to a particular credit customer for that month, together with any amounts outstanding from previous months. The statement also details any payments received from credit customers.
	Supplier:
	A statement that shows all the invoices and credit notes that have been received from a particular credit supplier for that month, together with any amounts outstanding from previous months. The statement also details any payments sent to the credit supplier.
Bank statement	A summary of transactions occurring within a given period for each bank account held.
Petty cash voucher	An internal document that details the business expenditure an employee has incurred out of their own money.

The process of recording bookkeeping transactions

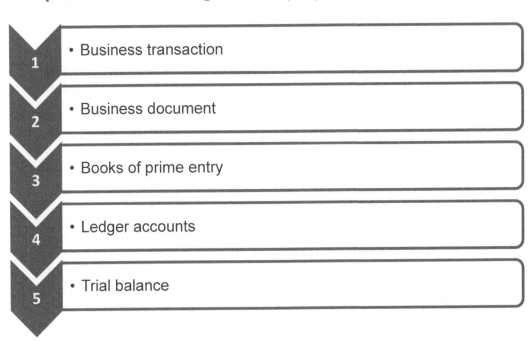

1. • Business transaction
2. • Business document
3. • Books of prime entry
4. • Ledger accounts
5. • Trial balance

- The transaction and details from the business document will be entered into the **books of prime entry**. A book of prime entry is where a transaction is first recorded. There are several books of prime entry which may also be referred to as 'day books'.

- The transactions that have been recorded in the books of prime entry are transferred into **ledger accounts** on a regular basis. Ledger accounts are used as part of the double-entry accounting system.

- A **trial balance** is a list of all of the ledger accounts in the accounting system and is used as a control to check that transactions have been recorded correctly in the double-entry system prior to the preparation of the financial statements.

- The **statement of profit or loss**. This is a summary of the business's transactions (income and expense) for a given period.

- The **statement of financial position**. This is a statement of the assets and liabilities of the business at a given date. This date is the end of the period covered by the statement of profit or loss.

- It is important to maintain accuracy when entering bookkeeping systems in manual and digital systems. Digital systems can import transactions from a number of sources.

- Ensure you know the benefits and drawbacks of using digital bookkeeping systems.

Create and use coding systems

- Coding is used within an organisation to provide an efficient and accurate way of referencing customers, suppliers, products and other accounts within the accounting system.

- There are different types of codes i.e. for a customer account, supplier account, product and general ledger accounts. Codes are used throughout accounting systems whether they are manual or digital.

- A code can be an alphabetical, numerical or alphanumeric identification system.

Set bookkeeping systems

- Double-entry bookkeeping is based upon three basic principles:
    - the dual effect principle
    - the separate entity principle
    - the accounting equation.

- Assets – Liabilities = Capital + Profit – Drawings

The accounting equation has limitations. Although we are able to calculate a profit figure, we are unable to determine the value of income and expenses. To be able to make this determination, we will now account for the movement in sales and purchases, rather than simply the movement of inventory.

Another limitation of the accounting equation is that in practice it would be far too time consuming to write up the accounting equation each time that the business undertakes a transaction. Instead the two effects of each transaction are recorded in ledger accounts.

We need to appreciate the effect a debit or a credit entry will have.

Ledger account	
A **debit entry** represents:	A **credit entry** represents:
• An increase in the value of an asset	• A decrease in the value of an asset
• A decrease in the value of a liability	• An increase in the value of a liability
• An increase to an item of expenditure	• An increase to an item of income (revenue)
• A decrease to an item of income	• A decrease to an item of expense

LO2 Process customer transactions

Calculate invoice and credit note amounts

- Understand the difference between total, net and VAT amounts and how to calculate them.

- Bulk discounts and trade discounts should be deducted before amounts are included in an invoice or credit note.

- Prompt payment discount allowed to customers (i.e. settlement or cash discount) is accounted for only when a customer takes advantage of the discount terms.

Enter customer invoices and credit notes into books of prime entry

- The sales day book is a list of credit sales invoices issued in date order, which records the transaction date, invoice reference number, customer name and account reference, along with the total, VAT and net amounts.

- The sales returns day book is a list of sales credit notes issued in date order which records the transaction date, credit note reference number, customer name and account reference, along with the total, VAT and net amounts.

- The discounts allowed day book is a list of prompt payment discounts allowed to credit customers which records the transaction date, customer name and account reference, along with the total, VAT and net amounts.

- Ensure that you understand, and can calculate total, VAT and net amounts based upon the following relationship:

	%	£
Net amount	100	500
Add: VAT amount e.g. 20%	20	100
Total amount	120	600

- Ensure that you understand, and can calculate total, VAT and net amounts, given any two of the three values in the relationship:

  e.g. net amount = total amount/120

  e.g. VAT amount = total amount/120 × 20

  e.g. total amount = net amount × 120/100

- Make entries in the sales day book as follows, with equivalent information recorded in the sales returns day book and discounts allowed day books as required:

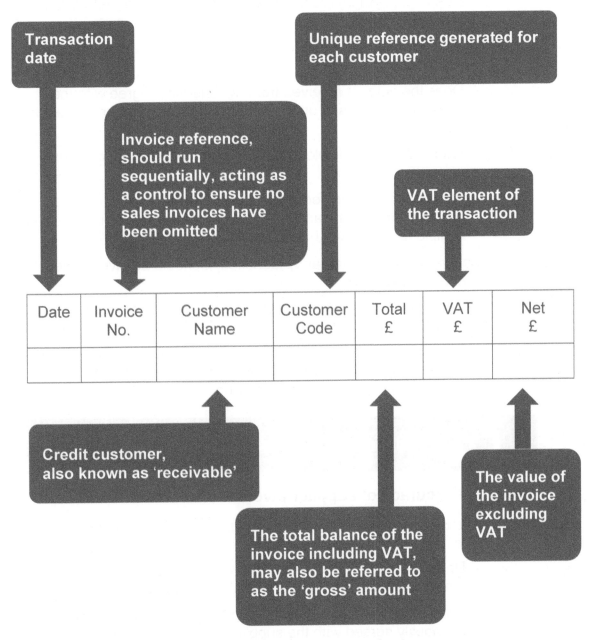

- Total the columns in the sales day book, sales returns day book and discounts allowed day book respectively and cross cast the totals to ensure that they are arithmetically accurate.

Process receipts from customers

- Details to check upon receiving a remittance advice include:

  - Does the payment received from the customer agree to the remittance advice?

  - Are all details on the cheque complete and correct so that it can be banked?

  - Does the amount received from the customer agree with the amount owing based upon their individual customer receivables ledger account?

  - Is the customer eligible to take any prompt payment discount offered?

  - If the customer has deducted prompt payment discount when preparing their remittance and making payment, are they eligible to do so, and has it been calculated correctly?

- In the event of any discrepancy identified, it should be investigated and resolved as follows:

  - If you have made the error, update or amend your accounting records as required

  - If the customer has made the error, contact the customer to advise them of their error and issue an updated statement showing the amount still outstanding.

LO3 Process supplier transactions

Check the accuracy of supplier invoices and credit notes

- Details to check upon receiving an invoice or a credit note from a supplier include:

  - Does the quantity and description of goods on the invoice or credit note match the goods actually received or returned?

  - Does the price charged by the supplier agree with what was previously agreed with the supplier?

  - Check that any bulk or trade discount agreed with the supplier has been deducted before calculation of the amounts stated on the invoice or credit note.

  - Check the calculations of net, VAT and total amounts on the invoice or credit note to ensure that they are arithmetically correct.

  - Check the date and terms of payment, including possible prompt payment discount, are correct.

- In the event of any discrepancy identified, it should be investigated and resolved as follows:
  - If you have made the error, update or amend your accounting records as required
  - If the supplier has made the error, contact them to advise them of their error and confirm how the discrepancy will be rectified e.g. a credit note will be issued or a further delivery of goods will be made by the supplier.

Enter purchase supplier invoices and credit notes into books of prime entry

- The purchase day book is a list of credit purchase invoices issued in date order, which records the transaction date, invoice reference number, supplier name and account reference, along with the total, VAT and net amounts.

- The purchase returns day book is a list of purchase credit notes issued in date order which records the transaction date, credit note reference number, supplier name and account reference, along with the total, VAT and net amounts.

- The discounts received day book is a list of prompt payment discounts received from credit suppliers which records the transaction date, supplier name and account reference, along with the total, VAT and net amounts.

- Ensure that you understand, and can calculate total, VAT and net amounts (refer back to the previous section if necessary) based upon the following relationship:

- The discounts received day book is a list of prompt payment discounts received from credit suppliers which records the transaction date, customer name and account reference, along with the total, VAT and net amounts.

- Make entries in the purchases day book as follows, with similar information recorded in the purchases returns day book and discounts received day books as required:

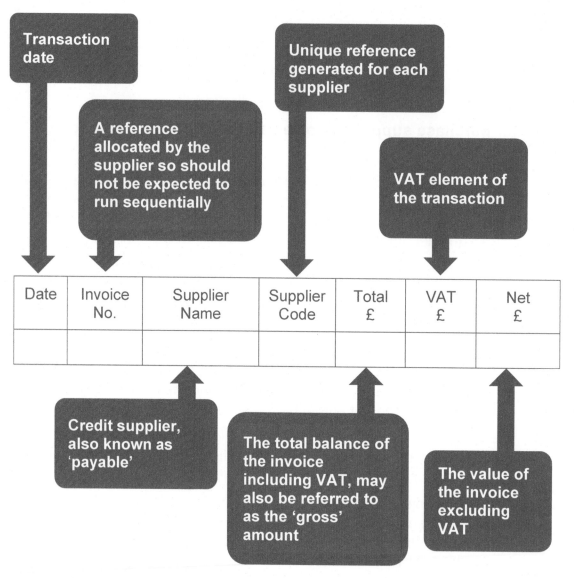

- Note that the purchases day book will often include analysis columns to analyse the net amount of each invoice into appropriate cost classifications and facilitate coding as preparation for posting of totals to the ledgers.

- Total the columns in the purchase day book, purchase returns day book and discounts received day book respectively and cross cast the totals to ensure that they are arithmetically accurate.

Process payments to suppliers

- Suppliers of goods and services on credit will usually send a monthly statement of account to each of their customers, detailing any balance outstanding at the beginning of the statement period, along with invoices and credit notes issued during the month, together with cash received and discount they have allowed to their customer.

- This should be checked against the payables ledger account for the supplier to ensure that it is accurate – any discrepancies should be investigated and resolved appropriately.

- Examples of discrepancies which may arise between the supplier statement balance and the individual payables ledger account for that supplier include:
    - cash in transit to the supplier, not on the statement
    - goods in transit from the supplier not yet received
    - discount or credit notes not yet accounted for by one party or the other
    - omitted or duplicated transactions.

- Many organisations use the supplier statement as a basis for identifying which invoices they will pay (e.g. all over one month old) or a responsible person within the organisation will decide which invoices should be paid.

- Before raising the payment, care should be taken to identify whether any prompt payment discount can be claimed and for that to be calculated correctly.

Appendix 2: Principles of Bookkeeping Controls

Introduction

This chapter recaps the key aspects of the Principles of Bookkeeping Controls unit.

UNIT LEARNING OBJECTIVES STILL RELEVANT FOR THE SYNOPTIC ASSESSMENT
LO1   Use control accounts
LO2   Reconcile a bank statement with the cash book
LO3   Use the journal

LO1 Use control accounts

Produce control accounts

Receivables ledger control account

	£		£
Balance b/d	X	Returns per SRDB	X
Sales per SDB	X	Cash from receivables	X
		Discounts allowed	X
		Irrecoverable debts written off	X
		Contra entry	X
		Balance c/d	X
	X		X
Balance b/d	X		

Payables ledger control account

	£		£
Payments to payables	X	Balance b/d	X
Discount received	X	Purchases per PDB	X
Purchase returns per PRDB	X		
Contra entry	X		
Balance c/d	X		
	X		X
		Balance b/d	X

VAT control account

	£		£
VAT on credit purchases	X	Balance b/d	X
VAT on cash purchases	X	VAT on credit sales	X
VAT on sales returns	X	VAT on cash sales	X
VAT on irrecoverable debts	X	VAT on purchase returns	X
VAT on discounts allowed	X	VAT on discounts received	X
Balance c/d	X		
	X		X
		Balance b/d	X

Reconcile control accounts

- Reasons for discrepancies between the control account total and the total of receivables (sales) ledger or payables (purchases) ledger balances include the following:

    - errors casting the day book totals posted into the control accounts

    - transactions omitted from the day books (and therefore, the control account also) but included in the ledger account balances, or vice versa

    - casting errors to determine an individual ledger account balance

    - omission or duplication of individual ledger account balances

    - debit ledger account balances classified as credit balances, or vice versa

- Note that some errors may affect the control account balance, whilst other errors may affect the total of the ledger account balances

- For reference, a specimen reconciliation of a receivables ledger control account, with the total of receivables (sales) ledger balances is below:

Receivables ledger control account

	£		£
Balance b/d	18,971.12	Discount allowed omitted	10.00
Undercast of SDB	1,500.00	Irrecoverable debt omitted	
			20.00
		Adjusted balance c/d	20,441.12
	———		———
	20,471.12		20,471.12
	———		———
Balance b/d	20,441.12		

	£
Original total of list of receivables ledger account balances	21,761.12
Duplicated ledger account balance	(800.00)
Adjust for credit balance initially included as a debit balance (i.e. 2 × £260.00)	(520.00)
	———
	20,441.12
	———

LO2 Reconcile a bank statement with the cash book

Payment methods

- Payment methods include:
  - cash
  - cheque
  - debit card
  - credit card
  - bank draft
  - standing order
  - direct debit
  - BACS (Bankers' Automated Clearing Services)
  - direct credit
  - CHAPS (Clearing House Automated Payment System)
  - Faster Payments

- Different payment methods affect the bank balances differently. A payment method might:
  - have no effect on the bank balance i.e. cash
  - reduce the funds within the bank account on the date of the payment
  - reduce the funds within the bank account at a later date than the date of the payment.

Use the bank statement to update the cash book

- Examples of items on the bank statement not initially recorded in the cash book include:
  - direct credits or BACS receipts
  - bank charges and interest
  - standing orders and direct debit payments.

Complete bank reconciliation statements

- The procedure for a bank reconciliation is as follows:
  - agree items on the bank statement that are also included in the cash book – tick off matching items
  - update the cash book for items on the bank statement but not in the cash book
  - update the cash book balance
  - prepare the reconciliation statement, beginning with the bank statement balance and adjusting this for outstanding lodgements and unpresented cheques.

BANK RECONCILIATION STATEMENT AS AT 30 JUNE 20X1

	£	£
Balance per bank statement		(1,160.25) O/D
Outstanding lodgement:		
cleared 2 July		6,910.25
		————
		5,750.00
Unpresented cheques:		
121 – cleared 5 July	538.00	
122 – cleared 3 July	212.00	
	————	
		(750.00)
		————
Balance per cash book		5,000.00
		————

LO3 Use the journal

Produce journal entries to record bookkeeping transactions

- A journal is a record of accounting entries which have not been in any other book of prime entry.

- Examples of journals used to record accounting transactions include the following:

  - accounting for irrecoverable debts

  - accounting for contras between the payables ledger control account and the receivables ledger control account

  - to record the opening entries for a new business

  - to record accounting entries relating to VAT and payroll.

- A proforma journal record is as follows:

Date	Ledger account name	Ledger account ref	Debit – £	Credit – £
31/12/X4	Wages expense	WE1	13,500.00	
	Wages control	WC1		13,500.00
Being recording of total wage expense for the month				
Date			£	£
31/12/X4	Wages control	WC1	10,000.00	
	Bank	CB1		10,000.00
Being net wages paid to employees				
Date			£	£
31/12/X4	Wages control	WC1	500.00	
	HRMC	HR1		500.00
Being tax-related deductions which are payable to HM Revenue & Customs				

KAPLAN PUBLISHING

Use journal entries to make adjustments in the ledger accounts

- A separate journal entry should be prepared for each transaction, including a brief note of the reason for the journal and reference to any supporting documents as follows:

Date	Ledger account name	Ledger account ref	£	£
31/12/X4	PLCA	PLA1	350.00	
	RLCA	RLA1		350.00
Being recording of contra between PLCA and RLCA				

Produce journal entries to correct errors not disclosed by the trial balance

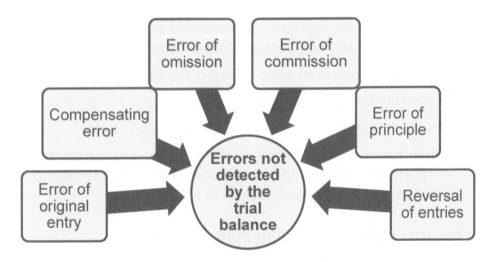

- Errors not disclosed by the trial balance mean that either no double entry has been posted, or that an equal value of debits and credits has been posted, but there is a problem with either the monetary amount and/or the ledger accounts used were wrong.

- The procedure to correct an error by use of the journal is as follows:
    - identify the double entry that was made
    - identify the double entry that should have been made
    - determine what double entry needs to be done to correct the error.

Produce journal entries to correct errors disclosed by the trial balance

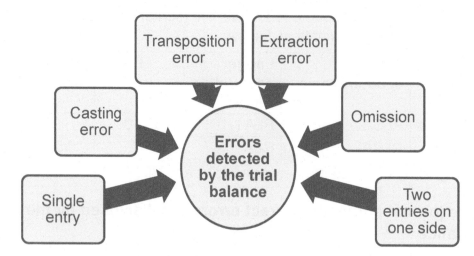

- Errors disclosed by the trial balance mean that an unequal value of debits and credits has been posted into the ledgers.

- The procedure to correct an error by use of the journal is as follows:

    - identify the double entry that was made

    - identify the double entry that should have been made

    - determine what double entry needs to be done to correct the error – note that one half of the double entry will be to clear the balance on the suspense account in this situation.

Redraft the trial balance following adjustments

- For any journal adjustments, whether to make accounting entries, or to correct errors whether or not they were disclosed by the initial trial balance, it is important to extract an updated trial balance to confirm that the value of debits and credits is in agreement.

INDEX

KAPLAN PUBLISHING

KAPLAN PUBLISHING